Learning
to
Fall

Learning
to
Fall

A Guide for the
Spiritually Clumsy

Timothy Merrill

Chalice Press
St. Louis, Missouri

Cover design: Dan Fruend
Interior design: Elizabeth Wright
Art direction: Michael Domínguez

This book is printed on acid-free, recycled paper.

Visit Chalice Press on the World Wide Web at
www.chalicepress.com

10 9 8 7 6 5 4 3 2 1   98 99 00 01 02 03

Library of Congress Cataloging–in–Publication Data

Merrill, Timothy, 1946–
    Learning to Fall: a guide for the spiritually clumsy/by Timothy Merrill
        p.   cm.
    ISBN 0-8272-2126-6
    1. Failure (Christian theology) 2. Christian life. I. Title.
BT730.5.M47 1998
248.4—dc21   97-50224
                                                          CIP
Printed in the United States of America

For Jeanie
Danielle, Jon, Debbie, Taylor, and Spenser

Acknowledgments

Writing can be a solitary enterprise or a collaborative one. In my case, there were many who helped me in this effort, bringing into focus both my meaning and the most effective way to express it. My wife, Jeanie, continually provided insights I had missed and was and continues to be the most significant influence for change and growth in my life. She has taught me how to fall and get up again—and has been a steady and encouraging voice throughout. I give thanks also to many friends who read portions of the manuscript or made suggestions when I asked for their input. These include Karen Rail, Keith and Norma Daly, John and Susan Hodin, Paquita Couch, Barbara Dalberg, Jerry Dalberg, and Steffon Dalberg.

Finally, thanks and a great debt of gratitude to my editor, David Polk, whose persistence has made this book possible.

Timothy Merrill

Table of Contents

III. How to Fall without Breaking Something Important

IV. Observations from the Chair Lift

I

Learning to Fall

1

Count It All Joy

Count it all joy when you fall into various trials.

James 1:2 (NKJV)

Falling is not one of my favorite things to do. I didn't like it when my parents took the training wheels off my bike, I didn't enjoy falling off a horse, and I wasn't wild about tumbling down a flight of stairs. I refuse to freefall from an airplane with the best of parachutes or dive off a bridge into the Royal Gorge with a rubber band around my waist. Call me chicken; call me a wimp. Just don't call me dead.

Yet, falling seems to grab the public's fancy. Were I to trip off the speaker's dais at a convention, it might trigger concern or laughter. President Gerald Ford, arguably one of the most physically fit of our presidents while in office, was nevertheless frequently ridiculed for the pratfalls he took descending the steps of Air Force One or while golfing with friends at celebrity golf tournaments.

The falls of life may take the form of financial disasters, or moral or criminal ones. One need only mention the names of Ivan Boesky, Charles Keating, Tonya Harding, Michael Milken, Gary Hart, Jim Bakker,

O. J. Simpson, Jimmy Swaggert, Richard Nixon, Leona Helmsley, and the entire royal family of Great Britain to realize "how the mighty are fallen."

Life is full of fallings. I believe it can be equally full of "gettings up"! Still, none of us wants to fall, and for good reason. Falling is dangerous. We might hurt something. We might look silly.

Yet, falling is not the problem. Everyone falls in life. The problem is that we don't do it very well. We have not learned to fall!

I realized this when my wife and I took the boys skiing. They were 9 and 7 at the time and had very little skiing experience. By then, Jeanie and I knew that it was much better to let someone else teach our children to ski than to attempt to do it ourselves. Fastening a screaming child into a harness and tugging him up a ski slope is fun for neither the child nor the parent. Equally dissatisfying is anchoring the child between our legs and snowplowing, which, while creating the illusion that the child is learning to ski, threatens to leave us permanently pigeon-toed—not to mention that we have no feeling in our legs. Christopher Buckley advises parents to ignore pain: "Try to ignore acute shooting pains in your lumbar region by focusing on the interesting new pain on the insides of your knees."[1]

We also tried the ski-pole method. We held a ski pole horizontally between us, to which we secured the child, and off we went. But after taking out a half-dozen people, catching them right in the small of their backs, mowing them down one by one, we abandoned this idea, too.

So we enrolled them in a ski school in Steamboat Springs, Colorado. When the boys didn't think we were watching, we listened and observed for a while.

The first thing the ski instructor did was to ask the nine-year-old to push her over. After hesitating briefly, he did as she requested. Down she went, ski poles, skis, and all. There she lay like a beached whale on a sea of snow.

Her point? We must learn how to fall if we're ever going to be good skiers. And we must learn how to get back up. The first technique this teacher taught was the fundamental technique of falling the right way. In her opinion, it was the most important aspect of getting to the larger goal of skiing well.

Wow! Her little object lesson snapped me to attention! Falling! I had never considered that learning to fall might be helpful. As I thought more about it, my entire attitude toward falling, risk-taking, courage, and success/failure began to change.

We're going to fall! That's all there is to it. So we might as well learn to do it right! We'll have those disagreements with our spouse, we'll get stopped for a moving violation, we'll experience challenges raising the children, we'll make decisions we wish we could recall. Every falling experience (call it stress) can be redeemed to prevent it from becoming outright failure! And this is what makes for true success: *time and pressure.*

When my family and I were in the occupied West Bank in the Middle East recently, we came across an olive press near Bethlehem. The olives were packed in burlap bags and placed in a large cement crucible where the oil was collected and from which it ran out into barrels. A long pole was fixed over a fulcrum and on the end of it were fastened large blocks of stone. The pole was adjusted so the weight of the stones rested upon the sacks of olives. Then, one waited for several days. For good oil, all that is needed is time and pressure.

In the Indian Peaks Wilderness area of Colorado, Ranger Jeff explained the same principle with a different metaphor. We were talking about the powerful force of glaciation, which had carved out the cirques and valleys of the spectacular Indian Peaks range. "A glacier develops," he said, "when snowfall in the winter exceeds snow melt in the summer." The subsequent buildup of ice creates tons of pressure that can move anything, given enough time—like thousands of years.

There it is! Time and pressure! Falls and stress can be positive forces for change. There isn't anything—whether rock, mountains, or valleys—that cannot be moved or reshaped if we learn to redeem our fallings before they become failures. This is precisely what James means when he says: "The testing of your faith produces endurance; and let endurance have its full effect, so that you may be mature and complete, lacking in nothing" (James 1:3–4).

Falling in life is only a confirmation that we are human. To redeem the fall is equally human; to give in to failure is to be less than human and to be less than what God has created us to be.

NOTE

[1]Christopher Buckley, "Shouts and Murmurs," *The New Yorker,* March 10, 1997, p. 100.

2

The Condo Cocoon

When I was in graduate school, I worked part-time on weekends as an X-ray orderly at a Presbyterian hospital in Denver, Colorado. During the winter months, the X-ray techs and orderlies always knew what would happen on Sunday evenings. Skiers would return from the mountains to be at their Monday morning jobs. Some of these skiers wouldn't make it to work. They had broken a leg or an arm, and these were the skiers we would see.

The patients, often bent over in excruciating pain, were wheeled into X-ray. When I developed the X rays and put them up to the light, I saw horrible compound and spiral fractures. I knew they faced six to eight weeks of rehab, time off from work and major inconvenience. Some of the injuries would put an end to athletic careers; some of the injured would never ski again, or not at the same competitive level.

I thought to myself: This will never happen to me. I don't want to break a leg. I don't even want to *risk* breaking a leg. To ensure my safety, I resolved to ski in control at all times. Better yet, I'd just stay in the condo at the base of the mountain in front of a warm fire with a good book.

Therefore, when I go skiing, I define success as never falling. I usually succeed because I never ski anything but the gentle slopes. Skiers whiz by me. But I seldom fall. Of course, I also never see the rugged mountain terrain, the blue and black trails; I don't experience the thrill that better skiers than I experience.

By staying in the condo or on the bunny slopes, I close myself off to a whole world of other possibilities. I don't fall, but my refusal to embrace the joy of falling makes me a victim of fear and limits my potential.

Time Out!

Perhaps we should define what we mean by the word *fall*. A search of the dictionary would reveal that the common understanding we have of *fall* is quite correct: it's a sudden, perhaps unexpected descent, plunge, decline from a high perch to a lower one. You get the idea.

Why does a fall create so much fear? Perhaps it is because we are afraid of physical injury and the pain associated with it. But often the pain goes away and the injury heals. Perhaps we are afraid of falling because we fear a loss of power. Our lives are no longer in our control. Events happen outside ourselves, and persons we have never met before are suddenly discussing our lives and bodies. And perhaps we fear the humiliating nature of the fall. When we fall, we often don't look so good; sometimes we look really silly and stupid. No one enjoys an experience like that.

Of course, we could discuss the concept of "fall" theologically. "In Adam's fall, we sinned all," reads the old Puritan primer. The fall of our first parents was a fall from grace, a fall from innocence, a fall from the will of God and the presence of God.

The New Testament understanding of sin has been explained many times. The word "sin" evokes the visual image of an archer shooting an arrow toward a target, only to watch the arrow fall flat on the ground well short of the target. When we "sin" in this sense, it's not that we fly wide of God's target, or even above and past the target. We don't have the moral energy to pull the bowstring back far enough to get our little arrow even close to the target.

Falling is something like that. We had dreams and aspirations, but rather than getting to the target and flying wide, our efforts have fallen miserably short.

The archery metaphor doesn't really work for me, since I'm not an archer. But I do golf. When I'm out on the fairway and am considering my second shot, I look up to the green and see the flag waving there about 160–190 yards away. Then I look down at my ball, sitting up nicely on the fairway. Suddenly, I have a vision of my next shot. I draw a three iron out of my bag and address the ball. I'm thinking of how beautifully the ball is going to take off, flying with a perfect, parabolic arch until it falls on the green in front of the hole. Then, if I jump up and down enough and yell, "Bite! Bite!" I know the ball is going to kick back, spin, and roll slowly toward the flag and in!

That's how it's supposed to work in a perfect golf world! It's much the same in our life with God and our relationships with others. We know what to do, and where we're going, and have nothing but the best intentions.

Thus, it is extremely frustrating when, after taking my second shot, I see a beautiful divot flying through the air and my ball dribbling up the fairway a couple of dozen yards. I'm not going to get par on this hole!

Woven throughout this discussion of what a fall is, one thing emerges, the one thing that defines both why we fear falling and the nature of falling itself. A fall is a loss of opportunity. In golf, I lose an opportunity to make par. I lose bragging rights!

If I fear falling because of physical injury, it is true the pain may leave and the injury heal. But it is also possible that I'll never walk the same, that there will be some concomitant effect that will render me unable to do things I had formerly been able to do. I fear *the loss of opportunity* to run, walk, talk.

This is precisely what happened to Christopher Reeve, of Superman fame. When he took that terrible, tragic fall from his horse, he lost a lot. We need not go over the details here. Although Christopher, his wife, and the doctors are hopeful that he will walk again, clearly his life has been changed forever; his fall was a loss of opportunity.

What Mr. Reeve has taught us, however, is how to redeem such falls. While the fall was a loss of opportunity, his redemption of the fall has created many other opportunities his pre-fall life would never have allowed.

If we fear the loss of power when we fall and have that aching sense that we are no longer in control, we are also the victims of a loss of opportunity. We have lost the ability, the opportunity, at least momentarily, to order and structure our lives. And until we recognize that the ordering and structuring of our lives is precisely the kind of business God is in, we will feel this loss keenly.

That's why, when my family goes skiing, fearing a fall, a loss of opportunity, I try to sneak off to the condo at the base of the mountain!

The Condo Doth Make Cowards of Us All!

Viktor Frankl, 91, a holocaust survivor and author of *Man's Search for Meaning*, argues that the difference between the sane person and the lunatic is that the lunatic believes that happiness is a right that life bestows upon its children. And if one does not possess it, rage and diverse psychosomatic symptoms result. Frankl observes that those who had the most difficulty in the concentration camps were those who believed that life owed them, that happiness was a right to which all mortals were entitled.[1]

The sane person is one who recognizes that there is at least one thing that no person or institution, however evil, can take away: the ability "to choose one's attitude in a given set of circumstances, to choose one's own way."

Condo dwellers, afraid to get out there on the mountain, ask: "What do I want from life. Why am I unhappy?" Frankl argues that a better approach is to ask: "What does life at this moment demand from me?" Happiness, he suggests, in pursuit of this agenda "ensues." It must necessarily happen.[2]

There is a real sense in which condo life, rather than producing *victors*, produces instead *victims*. Rather than protecting against failure, condo life leads inevitably to it.

Http://www.condo/cocoon.com

The human species is not created in such a way as to achieve greatness in the penultimate world of the condo at the base of the mountain. Personal growth or change must occur out in the world where reality is uneven and uncertain. Yet there is a growing impulse to retreat to the condo from the sensate world of rocks, ridges, and risks.

Trend guru Faith Popcorn calls this development "cocooning," saying that the phenomenon is characteristic of the more complicated, stressed, and dangerous days in which we live.[3] We are afraid of violence, and we prefer to avoid the hassle of interpersonal relationships at the office; therefore, we seek the comfort of the cocoon into which we have transformed our homes. With microwaveable popcorn, 500 cable channels, phone systems, computers, faxes, E-mail, grocery delivery services, television/movie/CD entertainment centers, a virtual and alternative universe can be created within the condo cocoon!

Popcorn notes that as conditions worsen outside, the virtual reality of the cocoon may become more desirable than the reality itself.

This is precisely the danger of the cocoon/condo: It is a desirable place to stay, but as appealing as it may be, it should never be thought of as permanent lodging!

Meet Curly the Caterpillar

Caterpillars do not use cocoons as humans do. For a caterpillar, a cocoon is a place of metamorphosis, which is a fancy way of saying change. In the natural safety of a cocoon, the caterpillar experiences change—radical transformation. It emerges later as a beautifully marked butterfly winging off to explore a world of flowers, blossoms, and trees.

Curly the Caterpillar does not say to himself while in the cocoon: "Cool! I sense I am really growing here! I can appreciate the changes in my life. Look at these fantastic wings. This is a good, secure place for me. So much is happening in my life. This is where I want to be. This is where I need to be. This is where I'll stay!"

Rather, Curly senses that that which is happening is only preliminary to even more startling achievements. Can you imagine Curly trying to organize the butterflies to campaign for stricter clean air standards? Curly is earthbound! The butterflies are Other Beings in a different world, a world he cannot appreciate; perhaps a world of which he is not even aware.

His failure to identify higher possibilities does not mean such a world does not exist. It simply means Curly is limited by his caterpillar nature. He will not be much else until he enters the cocoon, and—more importantly—leaves it. The cocoon life is penultimate; the ultimate reality awaits!

Dr. Leonard Sweet, dean of the theological school at Drew University, has a different, less negative view of the cocoon. He emphasizes the courage necessary to spin that cocoon, since it is, in fact, a chamber of death and metamorphosis.

For the caterpillar, there [is] nothing wonderful about [a co-coon]. A caterpillar doesn't just grow into a butterfly. A caterpillar must undergo molting and metamorphosis—the dramatic silence of the pupa in which the insect's morphology is entirely rearranged....A cocoon isn't safe. A cocoon is where a caterpillar risks it all—where it enters total chaos...where it dies to one way of locomotion and life and is born to a new way of living. A cocoon is where a caterpillar allows itself to disintegrate into a blob of gelatinous liquid without structure or identity so that it can emerge with sharpened sensory perceptions and breathtaking beauty.

Only in taking the risk of entering that inert pupa can the caterpillar go from dormancy to potency, from ugliness to beauty.[4]

Sweet goes on to observe that this is the reason the butterfly is such a powerful symbol of the resurrection! "Not because it's cute," he writes, "but because it risks dying to be born to new life."

Perhaps we prefer a more comfortable notion of "cocoon." Even in such a cocoon, Curly is less a caterpillar than he ever was before; but if he stays there, *he will never be what he was meant to be.* He's not what he was, but he's not yet what he will be! Therefore, the worst decision Curly could make would be to stay in the cocoon.

- Moses was safely cocooned in the court of Pharaoh when God called him to lead the Hebrews out of slavery.

- Siddhartha Gautama lived in the lap of luxury, protected by his father from all signs of disease, pain, and death. When Siddhartha saw by chance an old man, he answered the call to leave his protected environment, and thereafter he wandered the sub-Indian continent, teaching the Four Noble Truths and the Eightfold Path.

- Gandhi went to England to be educated and then forsook a promising career in law to lead his people to independence from the British.

- Martin Luther King, Jr., left the halls of academia and went from a pulpit to a prison in pursuit of his "dream."

Is it time for you to leave the condo/cocoon?

YOU KNOW YOU'VE BEEN IN THE COCOON TOO LONG IF:

■ You go to the video store and rent four movies for the weekend

■ Any one of those movies stars Sylvester Stallone

■ You know the real-life name of any soap opera star

■ You watch daytime talk shows

■ You have a toy poodle named "Precious"

■ You think "carpe diem" is a seafood entree

■ You think Moliere is a low-fat salad dressing

■ You have a friend with the nickname Bubba

Meet the Neoplatonists

Humans tend to reverse the metamorphosis. Whereas caterpillars enter the cocoon as caterpillars and leave as butterflies, humans enter as butterflies and leave as caterpillars. The tendency to entrench ourselves in our cocoon/condo inevitably leads to the loss of wings, loss of color, and loss of opportunity. It is truly a fall!

The Greek philosophers called this fall from butterfly to caterpillar a "loss of being." Early Christian theologians called this loss of being "sin." Neoplatonic (new Platonist) philosophers like Plotinus and neoplatonic theologians such as Athanasius and Augustine saw the moral universe as a hierarchical ladder upon which we climb toward Pure Being (God) or upon which we descend toward non-being. Wrong moral choices are choices against our very being. That is why we sometimes say that someone's behavior is "sub-human." We recognize that we have the capacity for acting in a manner that is less than human. It is possible, these philosophers argued, for humans to "fall" down the cosmic ladder of being, to live at lower levels of being than the Creator designed us for. Likewise, it is also possible to ascend the moral ladder of being by making the right choices.

That's why when we make bad choices, we often don't feel good about ourselves. We sense this loss; we know we have acted more like earth-bound caterpillars than sky-borne butterflies.

LEARNING TO FALL

Those who FAIL blame;
> *Those who FALL learn.*

Those who FAIL cannot tolerate the failure;
> *Those who FALL seek to understand why they fell.*

Those who FAIL say, "I need better equipment";
> *Those who FALL say, "I need better skills."*

Those who FAIL hate themselves;
> *Those who FALL love the experience.*

Those who FAIL say, "I'm not going to do this again!"
> *Those who FALL say, "I'll get it right the next time."*

Those who FAIL look down at the danger;
> *Those who FALL look up for a helping hand.*

Those who FAIL personalize;
> *Those who FALL analyze.*

Those who FAIL have an identity crisis;
> *Those who FALL have an inspirational crisis.*

Those who FAIL see how far they need to go;
> *Those who FALL see how far they've come.*

Those who FAIL stay down;
> *Those who FALL get up.*

Those who FAIL punish themselves;
> *Those who FALL reward themselves.*

Those who FAIL are victims;
> *Those who FALL are victors.*

Those who FAIL fail;
> *Those who FALL succeed!*

NOTES
[1]Viktor Frankl, *Man's Search For Meaning* (New York: Simon & Schuster, 1984), p. 140.
[2]Ibid.
[3]Faith Popcorn, *The Popcorn Report* (New York: Doubleday, 1991). See chapter 1 on Cocooning in which Popcorn refers to a cultural migration to the home as a haven against the world's dangers and problems. She argues that the cocoon exists in three forms: what she calls the armored cocoon, the wandering cocoon, and the socialized cocoon.
[4]Leonard Sweet, "Dare Care," *Homiletics*. April–June, 1997, p. 29.

3

You Can't Ski without a Slope

…because you know that the testing of your faith develops perseverance.

James 1:3 (NIV)

Many of us want a life without slopes. It doesn't work that way. With the slopes come falls, and with these falls—these "losses of being," these caterpillar-like moments—comes experience, and with experience, character, or what the New Testament writer James calls perseverance.

James is speaking about those who experience difficulties that arrive at one's doorstep uninvited. But we all know that many of our falls are brought *upon* ourselves *by* ourselves. Unfortunately, we not only court disaster, we usually send roses and engraved invitations! Is it possible to recover?

Ralph, 55, is ten years from retirement, is married, and is self-employed. A personable man of enthusiasm, he is well liked by family and friends alike. He has always been an outdoors man and has been saving money for fifteen years to buy a ranch and develop a program for handicapped children. On the advice of a close friend whom he trusted implicitly, he invested the bulk of their savings in a stock scheme. He was assured it was a low-risk, high-gain venture. His dream collapsed when it was discovered that Ralph's friend was part of a pyramiding scam, and the money invested had been reinvested in worthless paper and would never be recovered. Ralph feels even worse about this because he failed to confide in his wife about what he was doing.

"It's all my fault," he said to me when we met for lunch.

"Yes," I said.

"I'll never do something so stupid again."

"You mean you'll never take a risk again, or never keep something from your wife again, or never take someone's word again, or never invest without a complete investigation again, or never try to get rich quick again?"

Ralph paused and looked wounded. "I made that many mistakes?"

"No," I said. "It's not a mistake to take risks."

Ralph had a spectacular fall but was able to regard himself not as a victim, but as the beneficiary of a fall! He chose to regard his experience as a fall, not a failure! Today, six years later, Ralph has recovered some of his money through litigation, is saving and investing wisely, and is now ready to close on some acreage to see his dream fulfilled. Further, he and his wife have a new commitment that is enriching their relationship. The benefits of a "loss of opportunity" or a "loss of being," therefore, depend much upon our response to it. We can consider it a failure, or we can regard it as a fall.

Notice a few differences in these two ways of thinking:

Those who FAIL blame.
Those who FALL learn.

We're going to discuss how to learn from our mistakes in greater detail in chapter 15. But before we go on, let's remember that it is only natural to blame because blaming falsely promises to preserve one's self-esteem. If someone else is responsible, I don't have to admit that I screwed up. But there are harmful side effects:

• Blaming is self-defeating. Even if responsibility should
  properly be assigned to someone or something else, it is useless
  information

- Blaming keeps us from learning, thereby setting us up for the next failure
- Blaming gets us stuck in the past

On the other hand,

- Learning accepts responsibility
- Learning looks forward to another opportunity
- Learning focuses on prevention and preparation
- Learning allows the experience to teach

The success of Alcoholics Anonymous has been built on the premise that *causes are not deterministic.* Yes, alcoholism may have a basis in genetics; it may be a disease; it may have been brought on by an abusive home environment; and it may have been triggered by, for example, spousal abandonment.

So what? The issue is: What positive steps can one now take to be a victor and not a victim? Too many people stop after the problem has been identified. They feel that some sort of victory has been achieved because they have been honest about the problem and its causes. Discovery and honesty don't cut it. They are the necessary foundation upon which to build a new life, but with just discovery and honesty all one has is a foundation without a building.

"Fallers" will learn, not blame. "Fallers" take what Reinhold Neibuhr has called "responsibility despite inevitability."

Those who FAIL hate themselves.
Those who FALL love the experience.

It is typical to get angry at ourselves when we make a stupid mistake. Unfortunately, that anger sometimes spills over and affects others around us rather unpleasantly, not to speak of what it does to us. Anger is a poison that chokes the life out of our emotional and spiritual core. We may appear to be alive, but in fact we are "dead men walking."

Let it go and focus on the experience. You cannot change what has happened in the past; you can change only what is happening now, and you can chart a course for today and tomorrow. Celebrate what you can.

On the tombstone of Malcolm Forbes, yachtsman and publishing tycoon, are the words: "While he was alive, he lived." This is a variation of the Latin *Dum vivimus, vivamus*: "While we are living, let us live!" You, too, are alive; in this fall, you have tasted life.

Those who FAIL say, "I'm not going to do this again!"
Those who FALL say, "I'll get it right the next time!"

Failures prefer the subjunctive mood. "What if this were to happen?" they ask. They live in a conditional context: "Yes, we could do that, but this problem stands in the way." Failures also assume an attitude of omniscience. They know everything now. Ralph might have easily concluded: "My wife will never trust me again. What's the use?" Or he might have said: "I'll never trust someone again. What if I get fooled by someone else? The ranch for handicapped children was a nice dream, but I can't take another chance." He didn't lapse into the subjunctive "What if…" or the conditional "Yes, but…" of the omniscient self-pitier.

Instead, Ralph looked for help and found it in a compassionate and forgiving wife, and through the court system. Ralph learned to *use declarative sentences that objectify both the damage and the possibilities*:

- "This hurts."
- "This will take me x number of months (years) to recoup."
- "I will need a friendly banker and a good lawyer."
- "I need the support of my spouse."

Those who fall are willing to get help and are grateful for assistance when it comes. They remain optimistic about the chances for success the next time around. Like Grandmother used to say, getting her metaphors a bit confused: "When your wheels come off, get right back up on that horse and make lemonade."

Those who FAIL personalize.
Those who FALL analyze.

When we fall, invariably we begin to doubt ourselves. We may get so confused we hardly know how to dress ourselves in the morning. Making wardrobe decisions becomes an elaborate melodrama and an exasperating experience for those who have to live with us! We question who we are, and whether it is possible to know who we are. We

begin to think of ourselves as failures, no-good losers, miserable creatures with no future. Our confidence is shaken, the momentum is lost.

In the 1995–96 NBA basketball season, the Chicago Bulls, led by
Michael Jordan, Scottie Pippen, and Dennis Rodman, had an incredible season capped by winning the title in June. They lost a record low
11 games in the entire season! By February of 1996, they had lost only
three games when they arrived in Denver, where the Nuggets were having a very mediocre season. But that night the Nuggets handed them
their fourth loss of the season. The very next night the Bulls lost again.
Suffering that loss to the lowly Nuggets in a game they clearly were
supposed to win jarred even a superb, extraordinary team like the Bulls.
Confidence is so easy to lose. We can have a string of personal victories
and successes, but one failure can wreak more damage on the fragile
psyche we call our egos than all the successes we've racked up.

As we suffer questions of identity, we personalize the experience.
The rejection becomes personal—God is against us, the boss doesn't
like us, life has dealt us a bad hand. We slide into a pit of subjectivity,
unable to analyze what has happened. We take the event so personally,
we can't see ourselves, we can't see others, and we can't see what went
wrong.

Those who fall are able to find inspiration in even the darkest moments. They will not say that what has happened is a good thing, but
only that good can come of it. No situation is beyond redemption.
People who fall, rise up from the ashes of defeat like a phoenix inspired
to try again, to keep on living, to do it right the next time. They find
the courage inside to get it together and let the experience make them
stronger.

They can do this because they do not personalize; they analyze.

Analysis is a nonjudgmental process. It does not address questions
of how well or how poorly something was done. Instead, it seeks to
understand how things work, why they don't work, how this disaster is
put together, how it comes apart. Analysis seeks to understand the com-
ponents of an experience. It dissects, explores, investigates, mulls over,
attempts to discover and to learn. There's no time to cry in a beer.

There is no need to evaluate the experience you are tempted to call
a failure. That you use the word "failure" says that the evaluation of the
experience has already taken place. But those who have learned to fall
resist the temptation to personalize and instead analyze. They seek to

understand everything that happened, what went wrong, what went right, what was within their control, what was beyond their control. Frequently, such an analysis will reveal that there was nothing that could have been done to prevent the collapse. Such a revelation can be highly encouraging.

QUESTIONS FOR ANALYSIS

- What happened?
- How did it happen? Was it a random occurrence, an avoidable mistake, a case of enthusiasm getting the best of intelligence?
- Where did it happen? Does this affect only me? Have others been brought into this situation, and if so, what must be done to accommodate their needs?
- When did it happen? Did it happen when I was under a lot of stress? Was I preoccupied? Was I in a good place emotionally and spiritually?
- Why did it happen? Are the causes unknown? Is it a total mystery? If not, to what one essential cause can I attribute this "fall"?

When Thomas Edison invented the light bulb, someone asked him if he was discouraged after 1,000 attempts to produce a light bulb had ended in failure. He replied: "Not at all. The light bulb was simply an invention with over a thousand steps."

What step are you on as you re-invent your life? 504? 998? Or step 1?

Those who FAIL stay down.
Those who FALL get up.

When we are focused exclusively on the distance that remains yet to travel, we lose sight both of present and past progress. A goal fixation increases frustration when progress is momentarily impeded.

When I was a youngster, my dad took me hiking every year in Grand Teton National Park. There isn't a trail in that park that my hiking boots haven't plodded along. Occasionally, we attempted to climb a few of the smaller peaks in the area. One of these is Disappointment Peak. This rocky crag sits about 1,500 feet below Grand Teton itself. As one hikes the switchbacks up the shoulder of the Grand, one soon comes upon a couple of beautiful little lakes. From there, the view of the Grand is magnificent. In fact, it appears that one can begin an ascent up the far

PERSEVERANCE

- When he was seven years old his family was evicted from their home on a legal technicality.
- At nine, his mother died.
- At 22, he lost his job as a retail clerk. He had been trying to go to law school, but his grades weren't good enough.
- At 23, he went into debt to become a partner in a small retail store.
- At 23, he was defeated in his bid for the state legislature.
- At 26, his business partner died, leaving him a huge debt that took years to repay.
- At 28, after going out with a girl for four years, he asked her to marry him. She said no.
- At 37, on this third try, he was elected to Congress, but two years later he failed to be reelected.
- At 41, his four-year-old son died.
- At 45, he ran for the U.S. Senate and lost.
- At 47, he failed as the vice-presidential candidate.
- At 49, he ran for the Senate again and lost.
- At 51, Abraham Lincoln was elected President of the United States.

Some people get all the breaks.

cliffs on the western side of the lake and scale the Grand right to the top.

Indeed, this is what early climbers did. But they discovered, to their disappointment, that a huge, impassable gulf was hidden from their view. When they had climbed as far as they could, they stood upon the summit of a smaller peak, with the Grand still towering above them, absolutely unreachable. They called the peak Disappointment Peak.

I've often thought that we have a tendency to scale disappointments in our lives because we have set our eyes so obsessively upon the goal that we have lost sight of the journey itself and all that one must take care of while on a journey.

Failures whine about who they aren't, what they haven't accomplished, the raise they didn't get, the promotion that should have been theirs, the house they would like to have but can't afford. Often, this fixation leads to additional failures. We dive further into debt to have what we want and discover too late that it's too much. We may also find ourselves emotionally in debt, as well, with few reserves left with which to become emotionally solvent again.

Perseverance is a quality of all those who succeed. When falls occur, the perseverers get up; rather than wallowing in the angst of their suffering, they appreciate where they've been and how far they've come. While they understand that there is still ground to cover, they mix in a little patience with perseverance, enabling them, ultimately and inevitably, to succeed.

The word *perseverance* comes from a Latin root meaning to persist in an undertaking in spite of counterforces in opposition. Failures seldom persevere. Rather, they are stopped cold in their tracks. The ski patrol is called to carry their sorry bodies off the course and off the mountain. Fallers persist even in the presence of counterinfluences that mitigate against success. Fallers don't even understand the meaning of failure. For them, success is spelled p-e-r-s-e-v-e-r-a-n-c-e.

The National Hockey League recognizes the value of perseverance. The league has a "perseverance rating" in their stats for goaltenders. Factors such as total minutes played, goals allowed, and shots on goal are fed into a complicated formula that gives each goaltender his rating. In the 1994–95 NHL season, goaltender Hasek of the Buffalo Sabres had the highest perseverance rating at 980.92. The hockey pucks were flying, but he hung in there and deflected them more often than not.

The sports metaphor of perseverance is an apt one because one must be morally fit to endure the rigors of life. Living is not for the faint of heart, but for the great of heart. Blessed are the perseverers, for they shall succeed.

Those who FAIL are victims.
Those who FALL are victors!

The point here is that we are all victors; we haven't all secured the victory yet. *But the prize is ours; it only needs to be claimed.*

4

It's All Downhill

Success is not measured by how well or skillfully we climb the mountain; it is measured by what we do once we're there. People can usually get up the mountain; it takes considerable skill to get down.

Some people spend their lives attacking mountains. If a mountain is there, it will be climbed. The very presence of a mountain is an invitation for it to be conquered. "Come climb me," the mountain says. And we do. We fly thousands of miles to find a challenge. We pack tons of gear, engage the cooperation of governments, hire hundreds of the local population, risk life, and endure incredible hardships to get to the top of the world's highest mountains. Some don't make it. For every mountain, there is the story of those who have been killed trying to climb it.

A mountain, however, is a very poor metaphor for life. The good news is that life begins on top of the mountain, not at the base, as we have been led to believe. Think about it. For nine months, we are given a free ride to the top, and then comes the critical birthing moment: getting off the chair lift! Beginners often start the ride sprawled in the snow, squealing, and crying like newborn babies.

We don't look at life this way, do we? Rather, we go through life in an attack mode. We brace ourselves for what we regard as an incredibly difficult journey; we enlist the help of specialists—doctors, teachers, theologians, psychologists, therapists, parents, friends—to help us make it to the top. We gather all the equipment we think we'll need to make the operation a success—houses, cars, TVs, VCRs, computers, drugs, chemicals, vitamins, remote control devices. We do all of this for an experience at which we are not sure we'll succeed and about which we won't discover the meaning until it's all over!

I suspect this is why Thoreau went to Walden Pond. He didn't want to climb a mountain. Reacting against the prevailing wisdom, he chose instead a quiet, contemplative life, at least for a time, to learn more of life. He writes:

> I went to the woods because I wished to live deliberately, to front only the essential facts of life, and see if I could not learn what it had to teach, and not, when I came to die, discover that I had not lived. I did not wish to live what was not life…I wanted to live deep and suck out all the marrow of life…to rout all that was not life, to cut a broad swath and shave close, to drive life into a corner, and reduce it to its lowest terms, and, if it proved to be mean, why then to get the whole and genuine meanness of it, and publish its meanness to the world; or if it were sublime, to know it by experience.[1]

Thoreau here is quite willing to confront the "falls" of life. If life, when "shaved close" is a mean affair, Thoreau emphatically wants to know it and tell the world about it! He expresses no fear of falling, only anticipation and the calm assurance of ultimate satisfaction and triumph.

We need to get rid of the "mountain mentality." God gives us so much in life! It is ours to keep or lose! We have it all! But we insist on making such a task out of everything. For example:

Marriage. You and the one you are about to marry are standing at the altar. You are in love; you are in a friendship that is obviously working; you are in a relationship which is fulfilling. You have companionship, love, respect, and trust—you have it all! It is yours to keep or lose!

Why, then, do things so often turn sour? Could it be that we think that the easy part is over? Now the going gets tough. Do we think,

"This is as good as it's going to get?" In fact, are we not usually counseled that "marriage takes work to make it work"?

Let me tell you something: Marriage doesn't take work; marriage takes play.

As soon as the honeymoon is over you go off to work. You work at your job, you work at getting stuff, you work at going into debt, you work on the car, you work on the house, you work for the church, you work at your hobbies, you work to pay the bills. And then one day, you are surprised when your spouse looks at you and says: "Who *are* you? Do I know you?"

Marriage takes play, not work. Anyone can work. It's what we do best in this profit-driven, consumerist culture we live in. But we haven't learned how to play—together.

You say, "Okay, tell me how to play in my marriage."

It's incredible, isn't it? We are so grown up, we've forgotten how to play.

Think of the child playing in the sandbox. What is he doing?

1. He's being creative. Just look at what this child is doing! He's built roads and interstate highway systems. He's created mountains and valleys with roads and tunnels. He's fashioned castles and forts, and with a little water he's created a muddy lake. He's engineered an entire universe in a six by nine foot box of sand!

2. She's using her imagination. Children cannot play without imagination. It simply is not possible. Could you say to a child, "It's time to play now, but I'm afraid I can't allow you to use your imagination"? Someone once said of John Dryden: "His imagination resembled the wings of an ostrich: it enabled him to run, though not to soar."

Grownups run; children soar. Where does a child play? When a child goes off to play, she goes to a world of the imagination, a critical tool for play. The child sees things, hears things, knows things that can only be seen, heard, or known in the imagination.

3. He's doing something he wants to do. The child at play is a child who has set his own agenda. He is not playing to live up to the expectations of any other authority. He goes *where* he wants, *when* he wants.

I once watched our nine-year-old as he was finishing up a chore. He was supposed to feed and water our nine bunnies. He had finished watering, and so he shut off the water. It is a distance of about thirty yards from the faucet to the shed where the rabbit food is. On his way to the shed, he spied a stick on the ground. He picked it up and looked at it quizzically. Then he brought it to his shoulder, aimed it, and fired off several rounds in a number of directions, slaying an entire army of villains. By now he had wandered over to the picnic table, where he set the stick down and grabbed the barbecue skewer that was laying there. Suddenly, he jumped into a fencing posture. *"En garde!"* he snarled. He dashed forward with thrust and parry. He whirled and jabbed, he retreated and advanced until, in a furious exchange, he tossed his opponent to the ground and ran him through.

Leaving the skewer stuck in the ground, he picked up the stick again, fired off a few more rounds, and then ambled toward the shed. But wait! What is that by the fence? He saw an old towel that the wind had tossed off the picnic table. Grabbing it, he held it aloft and to the side to attract the attention of the bull. Ole! The bull charged, and only at the last minute did Spenser twist and escape being badly gored. The bull trampled past. Again the matador set himself. Again the bull charged. Again the flag waved and the bull charged past. Finally, grabbing the skewer, the matador showed the bull who was the master of the bullring. It was many minutes later before this child got to the shed and the bunnies were finally fed. We had set the agenda, but armed with imagination and creativity, this child could play only on his own terms.

4. He is not operating under a sense of time limits or constraints. See above.

5. She's doing what comes naturally. When a child asks if she can play, she is not seeking an opportunity to perfect the G major scale or load the dishwasher. How many times has a child said to a parent, "Mom, could I have some free time to clean up my room? It's been about a week since I've checked under the bed, and my closet is really a disaster"? Enough said.

6. He is at peace with himself. Children need time to play because while at play, a child is truly at peace and happy.

7. He may have a playmate. Some children prefer playing alone, but most enjoy the company of a like-minded friend.

Do you have a sandbox marriage? Is this a marriage you're working at, or playing at? Is it a marriage of creativity and imagination? Have you set your own agenda, or is it dictated by other authorities like, for example, your boss? or your in-laws? Does time intrude? Can you play happily with your life's companion?

The point here is that life is not a mountain to be climbed, but a view to be enjoyed. We spend more time *attacking* life than we do *attracting* life. When we are in the "work" mode, or the "grunt" mode, we attract death to whatever we are doing. The marriage—or whatever—becomes lifeless, dull, and sterile. When we affirm life, we attract life. Energy and vitality seem to flow again. Color comes back into the relationship, blood flows again to the extremities that were formerly lifeless. The very ground of our existence is soaked with the moisture of renewal! Take another example.

Parenting. A child is born. Do you think, "Oh, my! What am I going to do now? How am I going to get this child to maturity? How will we survive the challenges and difficulties? Where are we going to get the wisdom? How much will we need in a college fund?" We prepare to push this child as far as we can up the mountain. We sweat, groan, pray, strain, and struggle to get the youngster to age 18, an age at which we vainly believe the child will leave the nest and establish a life of her or his own.

Now let's look at this another way. The child is born. God has given this little person the incredible gift of life. And God has given you the awesome responsibility of parenting this life. Your task now is to gently *guide,* not push, this child down the mountain of life, exploring vistas, providing opportunities and training along the way.

Your job is not to "push" the child up the mountain. But this is precisely what many parents do with their children: push, not guide. Push them into the best schools; push them to be athletes and play some sport every month, every season of the year; push them to succeed—at something; push them to fulfill our expectations.

Millennial kids today are losing the one thing they should have—a childhood, some time to play on the top of the mountain. Today's parents, young Boomers or Generation Xers, insecure of their parenting skills, have their children everywhere but at home: they have them in school, after-school programs, sports, practices, piano lessons, dancing lessons, church, Scouts, camp, the day care, a job—everywhere, but not at home.

Life, then, begins on top of the mountain, and the journey of life—be it a marriage, career, parenting, or something else—is a perilous but thrilling adventure to the valley below. The difficult parts are at the top and middle sections. This is where the learning takes place, the experimentation, the victories, the rash judgment, the foolish excesses. By the time we have reached the base of the mountain, the terrain levels out, the throughways are expansive, and we can pick up speed. When we reach our senior years in life and have a few gray hairs, if indeed we have any hair at all, we find life a bit easier to negotiate; we've learned some important lessons, and we can speed on down the rest of the way to the valley.

In Hebrew scripture, a valley is often a symbol of death. "Yes, even though I walk through the valley of the shadow of death, You are with me," writes the psalmist. So life begins at the top of the mountain, and the journey consists of a course that leads to the eternal valley, our place of eternal rest.

Meet the French Existentialists

Therefore, life is not a climb! Let's throw away this old notion of life as an excruciating effort. Haven't we all enjoyed the cartoons that depict an exhausted climber struggling to reach the summit of a peak and when there, encountering a bearded guru who is supposed to dispense the meaning of life? "The meaning of life is…coffee." Or chocolate.

Albert Camus (d. 1962), author of *The Plague, The Stranger*, and other works, was a brilliant young philosopher of the French Resistance during World War II, and of the philosophical circles of post-war France dominated by Jean-Paul Sartre, Simone de Beauvoir, and others. In a smaller, less-known work titled *The Myth of Sisyphus*, Camus turns to Greek mythology to discuss the meaning of life. In this myth, Sisyphus is compelled by the gods to roll an enormous stone all the way up an equally enormous mountain. Such a task requires extraordinary strength and exceptional conditioning and results, understandably, in stress, fatigue, and discouragement.

When Sisyphus finally succeeds in pushing the stone to the top, the gods cruelly roll it back to the bottom of the mountain and demand that he push it up again. This, then, becomes his life: pushing the stone up, watching it roll down, and pushing it up again and again and again. Sisyphus was, for Camus, a symbol of the futility of modern life, which too often consists of meaningless and repetitive efforts. This is why in the opening lines of his book he argues that the only truly philosophical question is suicide. If this is life, then what compelling reasons exist for living it?

Of course, it is possible to reject a Sisyphyian model of life and still use a mountain as a metaphor for existence. But I reject even that. Life is not the arduous, exhausting climb of a mountain; rather, it is, or can be, an effortless and graceful journey toward our eternal destiny. Most of us will survive and reach old age. The force of biological gravity alone will help us tumble toward the valley. It would be better, however, if we could make this journey with some grace and flashes of style.

In Part 3, we talk about how to fall without breaking something important. But before we go there, we need to take a look at why we fall. What causes the tumbles we take on the slopes of life? We often fall because:

- we don't know what we're doing;
- we lose our balance;
- we turn stumbles into tumbles;
- we can't find the fall line;
- we have falling expectations;
- we suffer from falling phobia;
- and we are guilty of falling folly.

NOTE

[1]Henry David Thoreau, *Walden* (New York: Harper & Row, 1965), p. 67.

II

Why
Do
We Fall?

5

We Don't Know
What We're Doing

In Dallas, Texas, there is a single, young attorney, about 28 or 29, who lives alone in an apartment. Every Thanksgiving, it is customary for the law firm by whom he is employed to distribute turkeys among the employees, but this young man can never figure out what to do with his. Being single, he really doesn't want to cook the thing, and he could never consume all of it anyway. So every Thanksgiving it is a problem to know how to dispose of this bird. The distribution of the turkeys is always accompanied by a lot of pomp and ceremony. The president of the firm lines them all up on a table, and each person files by to get his turkey.

One Thanksgiving, some of this young man's friends decided to play a small prank on him, so they stole his turkey and replaced it with a bogus one made of papier-mâché. It was wrapped with brown paper and had just the neck and tail of the real turkey showing. They stuffed it full of newspapers and rocks to give it the proper weight. It looked for all the world like the others. The time came to distribute them, and when the president gave him his turkey, he accepted it gratefully and took it home with him on the bus.

He was sitting there with this thing in his lap when a man came down the aisle and sat down beside him. This man was obviously down on his luck, a little shabby, and run-down at the heels. They struck up a conversation, and the man told him what had happened to him. He had been hunting for a job all day but had had no luck whatever. He had only a dollar or two in his pocket with which to buy something for a Thanksgiving meal for his family. He was quite concerned because he knew his children would be disappointed.

Well, you never know when you're being fed a line, but as they chatted, the attorney became convinced of the man's sincerity. Then a light came on in his mind. "Here's where I can do a service for my friend," he thought, "and at the same time get rid of this bird." His first thought was to give him the turkey, but then he thought, "No, that might offend him. I'll sell him the turkey instead." So he asked the man how much money he had on him. The man said, "Two bucks." The attorney said, "I'll sell you the turkey for two dollars." So the transaction was made and both were very satisfied. The man got off the bus with his turkey, and the attorney went home with his money.

Imagine the scene when this unfortunate fellow got home with his two-dollar turkey. The children are gathered around the table, all excited, and they unwrap the turkey, and there is this phony bird. Let's not even think of the words that may have flown out of his mouth.

When the lawyer got back to the office after the holiday weekend and discovered what had happened, he was appalled. He and his friends rode the bus for a week trying to find this man again. They walked the streets and knocked on doors. They would have done anything to set this matter right, but they never found this man or the bogus bird.

In life, we fall sometimes simply because we do not have all the information. The lawyer didn't know what kind of bird he had, his friends had no idea that he would give it away, and the hungry man and his family could never know how innocent the lawyer was of the crimes of which they now accused him.

Gerontologists use neuropsychological predictors to determine the likelihood of falling among the elderly. One of the important factors in a large percentage of falls among senior citizens is cognitive impairment. In many cases, at advanced ages, the ability to assimilate information, process, and interpret it is impaired or diminished. Distances are incorrectly read, objects are not seen, and pertinent information is forgotten. Recent studies indicate that over 50 percent of the falls the elderly experience could be avoided by simply lowering bedside heights for better accessibility and installing seat belts on wheelchairs!

For the rest of us, avoiding falls is not simply a matter of lowering the height of our bed or snapping a seat belt. It seems to be a much more complicated issue.

A couple of years ago my son, Jon, and I went hiking in the Maroon Bells Wilderness Area not far from Aspen, Colorado. The trailhead begins not far from Maroon Lake; the Maroon Bells Mountains flank the lake on the far side. It is one of the most photographed sites in the world, especially in the fall when the aspens have turned into a blaze of gold. Now, however, we started out in midsummer. At the trailhead a sign is posted that reads: "Hikers beyond this point should be prepared for dramatic and sudden changes in the weather."

The sign that the wilderness rangers had posted offered me a new paradigm for living. In other words: *Life at High Altitude may involve Random Challenges and Radical Surprises!* It goes with the territory. Choices will be made. Timberline will be abandoned, alpine storms will be encountered, treacherous passes will be traversed, snow cornices negotiated, swollen, raging rivers forded.

With these challenges, however, come Radical Surprises: the explosion of wild flowers after the mountain rain, the clarity and range of vision, the scent of wilderness, the thrill of rugged and rare beauty.

As I read that sign, I committed myself again to accept the challenges and surprises of life. If I want to experience high-altitude living, I had better be ready for high-altitude challenges and high-altitude surprises.

Jon and I set out. We crossed a high mountain pass well above timberline, crossed a stream or two, and then, as afternoon wore on, headed into what appeared to be an afternoon shower.

We needed to make the next pass, about 12,600 feet. But it was a good 30 minutes away. Should we go for it or stop now and pitch our tent?

We stopped, and no sooner did we have the tent up, than it began to rain. It rained for thirty hours straight.

Now, my son and I have a good relationship. He was 16 at the time. Still, spending thirty hours in a small mountain tent with your Boomer dad is not exactly a Generation Xer's definition of a good time!

When, after thirty hours, it began to snow, we began to think of survival issues. We decided to "bug out." Attempting to go back the way we came was out of the question: the pass would be too treacherous after the rain. So we descended as straight as we could into the valley, following deer trails, and scree above mountain streams. We came out on a road along the Crystal River.

Opting to head for Crystal City and then Marble, where we believed we could hitch a ride back to Aspen, we set out. About two hours later, now late afternoon, the road swung into the river and out on the other side. But the river was so high and the current moving so fast, that it was unfordable. The risk of attempting to cross was too great.

We scouted possibilities upstream and downstream. But nothing presented itself. We were stuck. We pitched our tent and settled in uneasily, not knowing what tomorrow would bring forth. We had no idea how we would get out. Retracing our steps would mean an incredibly long hike, and an even longer (days) hitch back to Aspen. But, unable to cross the river, we had little choice. We slept fitfully that night.

The next morning was as clear and bright as the previous day had been gloomy and dark. Just standing in the sun with a cup of hot coffee in our hands made us feel better. But the nagging problem remained: returning down the long way we had come and hitchhiking a circuitous route around the mountains and back to Aspen.

While we were thus musing, we heard movement in the bushes nearby. Moments later, a small child emerged, followed by another and another. Soon, our little camp had a dozen children, all with packs, standing around. They were a group with Outward Bound, and their team leaders sprang into view after they were assembled.

We were glad to see them. Company was welcome, especially since we were in such a quandary. It was comforting to be able to share our misery. Apologetically, I approached one of the leaders and greeted him warmly. Then I said, "Too bad the river's uncrossable. We're just getting ready to head back."

I can't remember what he said. He was too busy unloading his pack to say much. The children all seemed busy. Their packs were on the ground, and they were all digging about for something. Then I saw one of them produce a pair of water shoes, small rubber slippers that slip over the foot, ideal for crossing streams with rocky bottoms where the footing is treacherous.

It didn't take the group long before they all had water shoes on and their other boots stowed. "Let's go," cried one of the leaders. A child went first. Down the bank, to the river's edge. He put a foot in the water, and then the other. After hefting his pack to just the right balance, he set out. Within minutes he was on the other side. Before he had arrived, another child was in the water, and soon, before we could say "The river's uncrossable," they were all over on the other side, stowing their water shoes and getting their boots back on. They waved Jon and me a cheery goodbye and disappeared down the road to Crystal City.

Jon and I were amazed. Actually, Jon was amazed; I was embarrassed. I am an experienced hiker. I should have known that the water in the river would subside after the rain had stopped. Yet, it never occurred to me to check the river again in the morning. I assumed that what had been true the day before would be true the day after, and the day after that. I had incredibly limited our options simply by refusing to reexamine the situation.

From this experience, I learned some lessons. I jotted them down later when we reached our car in Aspen:

- Everything looks better in the morning.
- The solution you want isn't always the best.
- The solution you want isn't always possible.
- What you want, if you had all the facts, you wouldn't want.
- Even when you think you have all the facts, you don't.
- Reexamine the options.
- Reexamine them again.
- Don't despise the obvious.
- Trust the map.
- Little pebble in boot cause big blister on foot.
- Never take shortcuts.
- Find a good pace and stick to it.
- Travel light.
- Be prepared for the long haul.
- Keep the matches dry.
- Man (and woman) shall not live by freeze-dried foods alone.

We fall because we don't know what we're doing.

6

We Lose Our Balance

Here in Colorado we have some of the best, if not the best, skiing in the country, even the world. When I talk to expert skiers, the issue of balance is continually mentioned. Skiers fall when they are "out of balance, or out of center."

The physiological problems associated with a sense of balance are also a big factor in the spills the elderly frequently suffer. Clearly, a good sense of balance is important in all phases of life: physical and recreational—and emotional and spiritual.

If one had a smooth surface on which to walk, losing one's balance might still be a problem. When, however, as with skiers, the surface is not smooth but bumpy and slick with a downhill angle, maintaining balance is a difficult challenge. Novice skiers tend to overcompensate and lean either too far forward or too far back on the skis. In either case, a fall is likely to occur.

The life paradigm is obvious and does not need to be overstated here. Life is a graded slope of varying levels of difficulty and stresses. Leaning forward, backward, to the left, or to the right, we are candidates for a spectacular, sprawling collapse.

What Causes an Out-of-balance Condition?

The irritating reality is that anything can cause you to lose your balance: a chunk of ice, a rut, catching an edge, looking up, looking down, looking at someone else, looking at yourself. Sun glare, wind, and snow. Colliding with another skier will cause you to lose your balance. Running into a tree, thinking about running into a tree. You can lose your balance for no apparent reason: One moment you are cruising; the next you're face down in the snow.

It is not difficult to diagnose these moments of imbalance. When you're spitting out snow and ice, shaking it out of your cuffs and collar, feeling the snow cold and clammy at the base of your neck on its way down your back, you know that something has happened. You're irritable, depressed, cranky. You don't have enough time to get everything done. The routine of your life has taken on an empty, meaningless quality. Other family members are beginning to notice the snow in the cuffs and collar. They offer to help you brush it off. They are unusually kind and solicitous. They're treating you as a sick person. You feel sick. You're not yourself. Your spouse keeps asking, "Is everything okay?" The kids are avoiding you. The cat is avoiding you. You're aware of how little help you are getting from others. You are conscious of how inconsiderate others are.

It's a Cosmetic Problem

The Greeks gave us the word *cosmos,* from which our word "cosmetic" comes. When a woman gets up in the morning, she is likely to use a variety of cosmetics before she heads out the door for work. Men have their own preening rituals as well, but cosmetics do not play as large a role, if indeed any role at all. A woman usually has an arsenal of ointments and powders that she applies to her face every morning. The process goes like this: She looks in the mirror at her face (a morning face, be it a man or a woman, is often not a pretty sight). The face is her cosmos and she sees, to her horror, that her cosmos is in total chaos or at least significant shambles. To bring order out of chaos, she applies mascara, rouge, highlights, lipstick, eyeliner, and so forth. Soon, the facial cosmos is ordered as it should be, and she is ready to face the world!

I sincerely am not making fun of this exercise! This is precisely why these unguents are called cosmetics. For a cosmos in which everything was in its place and there was a place for everything was very important for the Greeks. The essence of Plato's theory of government is that the good citizen must find his niche in life: cobblers should cobble shoes, rulers should rule, and teachers should teach. Anything else is chaos.

Chaos in the Cosmos

Chaos is not good. Few of us care for it much. Yet, as much as we dislike chaos, we seem to invite its presence in our lives, or—if not invite, at least allow it to set up housekeeping. When people were surveyed about the stress in their lives, these answers occurred repeatedly. We struggle with:

- money problems
- housekeeping
- finding "me" time
- teenagers
- communication
- overscheduling
- volunteering
- our work situation
- self-image
- our spousal relationship

- guilt for not getting stuff done
- family members
- dieting
- television
- moving
- neighbors
- in-laws
- the new baby
- children
- and more.

When we feel cosmic chaos, we know that it is time to do something. But what? We are not interested in something merely cosmetic and superficial.

Have an Argument

The word *argue* comes from another Greek word related to *argent,* meaning "silver" or "white" (compare *Ag,* the chemical abbreviation for "silver") or denoting brilliance and clarity. The word has its basis in the mythology of Argos, the creature with a hundred eyes. When Hera, the wife of Zeus, suspected her husband of having an affair with a nymphet called Io, he changed Io into a cow. But Hera, suspecting what he had done, had Argos stationed to guard the cow to ensure that Zeus would not change her back into the beautiful Io. As the story goes, Io, as a cow, escaped, and the Bosphorus (the ford of the cow) and the Ionian Sea are named in her honor.

When there is chaos in our cosmos, an argument—that is, a discussion that enables us to see clearly, as though we, too, had a hundred eyes—can be extremely helpful. Such a discussion will enable us, in these chaotic moments, to clarify the issues and identify possible solutions and outcomes.

DAR® : A Three-Step Matrix for Banishing Cosmic Chaos!

Step One: Deconstruct

Deconstruct your life as a way of identifying what your life is made of. Take it apart piece by piece. Look at each piece, turning it over, gazing at it from every possible angle, and slot it into *Role, Relationship,* or *Reward*.

Roles: You have specific roles in your emotional, spiritual, professional, social, marital, and familial life. Your role list could look like this:

Nurturer	Facilitator	Teacher
Fixer	Referee	Healer
Giver	Protector	Friend
Lover	Driver	Leader
Cook	Maid	Appeaser
Caregiver	Supporter	Encourager

These, in turn, should be slotted into broader roles that define your life. The previous list of roles could now look like this:

Emotional	**Spiritual**	**Professional**
Nurturer	Nurturer	Facilitator
Caregiver	Caregiver	Teacher
Appeaser	Appeaser	Fixer
Supporter	Healer	Leader
Encourager	Supporter	Referee, etc.
	Encourager, etc.	

Marital	**Social**	**Familial**
Healer	Friend, etc.	Protector
Giver		Cook
Lover, etc.		Maid, etc.

Any one of the roles on the master list can be slotted into the major categories by which you define your life. The more frequently these roles appear, the stronger your stress.

Moreover, these are active roles. These roles require you to "do unto" not to be "done unto." You are asked to be the nurturer, not the nurtured, the lover, not the loved. Being loved is not a role one plays; it is a blessing one receives.

Relationships: Next, deconstruct your life in terms of the people in your life:

Husband	Wife	Child
Neighbor	Mother	Father
Boss	Employee	Friend
Coworker	Sibling	Family member

Rewards: Finally, deconstruct your life by identifying the rewards that are important to you. They may be intrinsic or extrinsic things that give you pleasure from your performance in your role(s):

Love	Self-esteem	Pleasure
Respect	Fame	Money
Happiness	Security	Actualization
Comfort	Fulfillment	Admiration
Nurturing		

Step Two: Assess

Assess your relationships in terms of the role you play and the rewards you gain. Your life is out of balance if:

- The number of **roles** you play in a given **relationship** outnumbers or outranks the **rewards** you gain; or
- If the **roles** you play are inappropriate for the **relationship**.

Consider the chart on the top of p. 41:

This woman feels that she plays many different roles in relationship to her husband but derives very little for herself from the relationship. Clearly, she is face down in the snow, extremely upset with her clumsiness.

ROLE You are the:	RELATIONSHIP For your:	REWARD And are rewarded with:
Nurturer	Husband	Love
Facilitator	Wife	Self-esteem
Teacher	Child	Pleasure
Fixer	Neighbor	Respect
Referee	Mother	Fame
Healer	Father	Money
Giver	Boss	Happiness
Lover	Employee	Security
Driver	Friend	Actualization
Builder	Sibling	Fulfillment
Leader	Family	Admiration
Cook		Nurturing
Maid		

Step Three: Recalibrate

Now create a fourth column in which you describe the recalibration that the relationship must experience before your life is centered and balanced again. Your chart could look like the one on p. 42.

The recalibration column accomplishes several things: It allows you to take control of a situation you feel is wildly out of control, a feeling not uncommon when life is out of balance. It also identifies possible responses to aggravating circumstances. It establishes the principle that every relationship inevitably needs periodic adjustment, however minute, in order for it to be a relationship that not only functions effectively but is rewarding as well.

Relationships are like washing machines: when the load is off center, they start making loud thumping noises and begin lurching across the room bumping into things. Relationships can take awfully heavy loads, but they must be balanced. Recalibration is the process of shifting the load so that the noise and lurching stops, and the equipment functions as it was designed to function.

ROLE You are the:	RELATIONSHIP For your:	REWARD And are rewarded with:	RECALIBRATION Thus, I must:
Nurturer	Husband	Love	Be honest
Facilitator	Wife	Self-esteem	Be assertive
Teacher	Child	Pleasure	Get angry
Fixer	Neighbor	Respect	Explain
Referee	Mother	Fame	Write a letter
Healer	Father	Money	Take time off
Giver	Boss	Happiness	Share feelings
Lover	Employee	Security	Get tough
Driver	Friend	Actualization	Show patience
Builder	Sibling	Fulfillment	Accommodate
Leader	Family	Admiration	Join a support group
Cook		Nurturing	Set aside time
Maid			Develop schedule
Appeaser			Look elsewhere
Supporter			Withdraw support
Encourager			Reaffirm support
			Modify role
			Withdraw from role

What is Your Mission Statement?

Shifting the load is another way of stressing the importance of our "cosmic center." Such a center is found in the spiritual, not the material realm.

Viktor Frankl, author and psychiatrist, says that when people come to his clinic overburdened with problems, the staff often ask them: "Why not commit suicide?"[1] In the answer to that question lies the hope of recovery from the depression or malaise with which the patient is afflicted. They do not commit suicide because of a close family relationship, or because of a project they'd like to finish, or because they have memories that they'd like to preserve. By locating these reasons for living, Frankl is able to help his patients put together again the tattered fabric of their lives.

Frankl is someone who knows about the difficulty of discovering meaning and purpose in life. Gordon W. Allport, one of the most significant interpreters of Frankl to American psychologists writes:

> As a longtime prisoner in bestial concentration camps [Frankl] found himself stripped to naked existence. His father, mother, brother, and his wife died in camps or were sent to the gas ovens, so that, excepting for his sister, his entire family perished in these camps. How could he—every possession lost, every value destroyed, suffering from hunger, cold, and brutality, hourly expecting extermination—how could he find life worth preserving? A psychiatrist who personally has faced such extremity is a psychiatrist worth listening to.[2]

Frankl writes that when he was in the concentration camps during the war, prisoners would hoard coupons they occasionally received in order to exchange them for cigarettes that could then be exchanged for soup. Those comrades who had lost the will to live, however, kept their cigarettes and smoked them. "Thus, when we saw a comrade smoking his own cigarettes, we knew that he had given up faith in his strength to carry on, and, once lost, the will to live seldom returned."[3] He would be dead within days.

Some of us have decided to smoke our cigarettes. Our lives are so hopelessly out of balance, out of control, out of center, that the meaning and purpose of life is totally lost to us. Yet, there is a center, a focal point around which we gravitate like moths to light. We have simply forgotten what it is, or neglected it.

Finding the center of our lives is nothing more than developing a personal mission statement. The apostle Paul shared his when he wrote to his friends at Philippi:

> Yet whatever gains I had, these I have come to regard as loss because of Christ. More than that, I regard everything as loss because of the surpassing value of knowing Christ Jesus my Lord. For his sake I have suffered the loss of all things, and I regard them as rubbish, in order that I may gain Christ and be found in him. (Philippians 3:7–9a)

Notice how easy it is to impose the **DAR®** approach in this passage in Philippians. Paul begins by **deconstructing** his life in terms of roles, relationships, and rewards. He is a righteous Jew of the tribe of Benjamin, and so forth. He describes his relationship with the Philippians, his enemies, and Jesus Christ. He speaks of earthly and spiritual rewards. He then assesses it all, concluding that the earthly rewards are but garbage lost for the spiritual rewards he has in a relationship with Jesus Christ. Finally, he is determined to recalibrate lest he forget what is important: He resolves to forget what is behind him (the past) and press on to the "heavenly call of God in Christ Jesus" (13, 14). At that, Paul, having identified the center of his life, is able to **prioritize**: "I regard everything as loss because of the surpassing value…" He is also able to **suffer loss** and put that loss in perspective.

Recover Your Spiritual Center

There are three ways we can recover our spiritual center.

- **Write a mission statement.** To do this, begin freewriting by finishing the following sentence starters:

    "I believe that…"

    "I am…"

    "I have been…"

    "I am going to…"

When you have finished writing, develop a personal mission statement from your responses. It may take the form of a prayer or a letter.

- **Commit** by sharing your thinking with someone else.

- **Ritualize.** Rituals are repetitive experiences that symbolize your commitment.

Traditions that express your commitment to the changes you have ordered in your life will enable you to recover the balance a spiritually clumsy person needs!

NOTES

[1]Viktor Frankl, *Man's Search For Meaning* (New York: Simon & Schuster, 1984), p. 7.
[2]Gordon Allport, preface to *Man's Search For Meaning*, p. 7.
[3]Ibid.

THIRTY-FIVE RITUALS

Get up at 5 a.m. to read or pray
Have champagne on anniversaries
Call your mother every Sunday
Write in a journal every day
Memorize a verse from the Bible every day
Say the Lord's Prayer
Meet a friend for lunch on a regular basis
Attend a concert once a month
Pick a favorite meeting spot
Faithfully attend a discussion group
Attend your house of worship regularly
Compliment three people every day
Spend an hour a day gardening
Bake a loaf of bread Saturday mornings
Spend time with a grandchild regularly
Memorize poetry or scripture
Have pizza on Saturday nights
Buy yourself flowers once a month
Find a secret place in the park
Open a bottle of wine on special occasions
Write a poem on Monday mornings
Develop correspondence with a distant friend
Say "I love you" every day
Walk the dog
Run 2–3 miles every day
Take an early morning walk
Refinish a piece of furniture
Attend a movie on the first Wednesday of the month
Listen to music
Sing in the choir
Take a warm bath on Sunday nights
Volunteer
Make his favorite dessert
Give to charitable causes
Actually smell the coffee

7

We Turn Stumbles into Tumbles

Are you a "tripper"? I am. Trippers are those people who can stumble over a fleck of dust. It doesn't matter how minute the protrusion, if it's there, I'll trip over it.

God understands that we are by nature "trippers." That's why we're called the "sheep" of God's pasture. Sheep are not known for their athletic ability. They're rather clumsy animals. In fact, not long ago, assistant interior secretary George Frampton told a Senate subcommittee that "ovine ineptitude" kills 1,000 times more sheep in Montana than wolves. He describes the curious malady as "sheep who just fall over and can't get up."

President Ford was a famous tripper. Arguably the fittest president in the history of our great country, he tripped over everything and anything. He fell off Air Force One, off the first tee at the Arlington Golf Course, down the stairs, up the stairs; he was the best.

46

Politicians seem to trip a lot. President Clinton's leg and knee spent several weeks in a cast in 1997 as the result of a trip; Bob Dole tripped off a platform and into the crowd on the campaign trail in 1996.

Actually, tripping happens to everyone. We trip over the merest rise in the pavement, objects in the bedroom, an uplifted corner of the rug, or a root in the ground.

Usually we can recover when these trips occur; the arms go out for balance, we step quickly with the other foot, and we land safely. We then take a quick, annoyed glance backward at what we tripped over, amazed that such an insignificant object could cause such a violent adjustment in our stride.

Trippers are those who seem to have inordinate difficulty in staying on their feet when confronted with even the slightest difficulty. Every little obstacle, interruption, or unforeseen event becomes a major crisis. And if it is not a major crisis, the tripper finds a way to turn it into one.

Keeping Stumbles from Becoming Tumbles

There are some preventive steps we can take to reduce the tripping:

Watch where you're going.	Set goals.
Stay awake.	Establish priorities.
Pick up your feet.	Obey the rules.
Plan ahead.	Make good decisions.
Make lists.	Do what is right.
Communicate.	

We will trip, however. What can we do when that happens?

React immediately.	Move on. Let it go.
Remove the obstacle.	Laugh.

Don't over-dramatize the experience.

It's helpful to look at irritating situations as if you are watching your life as a sitcom on TV. There are more laugh lines than you might think. You're standing at the water cooler in the office having this stupid argument. Stop for a second and listen to yourself. There is a silent audience out there who finds your little drama hilarious. See life for what it is. *Your life is a sitcom, not a soap opera.* Avoid the hysterics and melodrama. There is no organ music playing in this scene, just an audience—and they're laughing.

Phone Calls

Jon and Lori came into my office one cold fall day almost, but not quite, convinced their marriage was irretrievably broken. As with many problems in relationships, communication was a factor here. In this case, we discovered that this crisis had developed from a simple failure to pass on some important phone messages. Lori felt her issues were not regarded as important by Jon, and Jon accused Lori of being excessively sensitive. Some simple adjustments were made to expedite receiving messages; both Lori and Jon reaffirmed their respect for each other, and each acknowledged they had been careless and inconsiderate, and they agreed to move on.

Not all problems are so easy to handle! In Jon and Lori's case, this small irritant had created larger ones. Many so-called "crises" in relationships emerge from the small stuff. Couples often find it easier to handle the major emergencies in their lives than they do the small, frustrating events that trip them up during the day.

Fast Tango in Paris

There is an old saying that if you want to really know someone, spend a vacation with him (or her). If your relationship survives a vacation, it will survive the marriage. I know of no studies to support this claim, but it makes sense.

My family and I have recently returned from a five-month sabbatical. It began in Paris. Ten days into this 150-day adventure as a family of four, we had a very bad day. It started when I insisted we find a phone to make a weekly call to the States. I rushed us through lunch. My wife tried to conceal her irritation, but I could sense something was wrong. We were definitely "tripping." Rather than reacting immediately to regain our relational balance and move on, we ignored it and, as a result, we piled on more and more misunderstandings and irritations throughout the day.

She wasn't feeling well, and the youngest child, 7, fell and scraped his chest and for a solid hour screamed bloody murder. We trudged to the Rodin museum where we had a silly argument over whether the "Thinker" in the courtyard was the original, or whether the original was elsewhere. By 5 p.m. when we finally arrived back at our hotel in the 2nd arrondissement, our "stumble" had become a major tumble.

After sending the boys up to the room, we began a fast tango outside the hotel on the rue de Leopold Bellan.

"Can we do this?" she asked, with tears in her eyes. I pretended not to understand what she meant, scrambling for an answer.

"Do what?" I asked.

"Do this—for five more months?" I dropped the charade, realizing what a cad I had been for the whole day. We also realized we needed to have time for ourselves each day so that agendas, planning, and relational issues could be mutually considered. That evening, we left the boys, 9 and 7, in the hotel room watching French cartoons, telling them we would be back in 90 minutes. We found a sidewalk café nearby and, over white wine, glanced back at the obstacles that had tripped us up, had a good laugh, and moved on.

In the five months we were together—day in and day out—we had only one other day like that fast tango in Paris.

8

We Can't Find the Fall Line

There's a lot I don't know about skiing. The first time I heard of the fall line I laughed because from my point of view I live and die on the fall line every day of my life! My brother-in-law, Jerry Dalberg, tried to explain it to me. The fall line is an imaginary line that extends from the top of the mountain to the base, and it is this line that a skier follows on the trip down the mountain.

Most skiers. My technique is to traverse the fall line, to waffle back and forth on the fall line in a criss-crossing sort of pattern. This seems much safer to me than skiing directly down the mountain at speeds I cannot control and over terrain that seems to invite certain catastrophe. Let Jerry ski the fall line if he so chooses, but let me go back and forth until at long last I reach the gentle slopes of the valley beyond and cease from my labors and enter into the joy of my eternal abode!

I have labored under a misunderstanding, however. It is not necessary to *follow* the fall line, but it is necessary to *face* the fall line. My problem—I'm told by those eager to point out that I have a problem— is that when I ski I do not face the fall line. My body, when I make my turns, shifts away from the fall line. The secret is to keep the upper body facing the fall line even as the skis may be—and usually are—doing something entirely different.

This seems risky to me.

There are two issues here: ignore-ance (as in avoid-ance), and death.

"Ignoreance"

Ignoreance, a nominal neologism based on the verbal "to ignore" (and pronounced ig-NORE-ance) is the willful decision to ignore or avoid potential for failure. When I am skiing, I am very much into "ignoreance." By turning my body away from risk and danger, I ignore, perhaps in an attempt to indefinitely avoid, the potential for mistakes and problems. Ignoring can be a successful strategy for conflict resolution, but the cases in which it is used are rare; more frequently, ignoring is a device to avoid the fall line that life inevitably forces us to face.

We ignore problems because (1) We are naive! Do I really think if I keep skiing laterally across this slope I can get down the mountain, avoid the fall line, and save myself? Ha! Right! We think these problems may go away by themselves. If we look away from the mess, the next time we look it will be gone. If we close our eyes, we may be able to convince ourselves it is all a dream. If we bury our head in the sand, the dark reality of having one's head in the sand may be preferable to the even darker reality of life above the sand.

The problem with all of this is that the mess never disappears—it only gets messier, the dream turns into a nightmare, the sand only grinds our eyes and our vision into a blur, and if I don't turn now, I'm going to hit a tree.

We ignore problems not only because we are grossly naive, but (2) because we are codependent. We actually think someone else will take care of them for us. If I leave my socks in a heap on the floor, perhaps someone—I wonder who?—will come through and pick up after me. If I wait this out and treat these behaviors as a "phase," perhaps they will phase out and disappear. If I let the work sit on my desk, someone else will get to it. If I avoid responsibility, someone will take care of it if it is really important. I'll just fall now right here in the snow and let someone else help me up and get me turned around, and then I'll ski across the fall line over to the next tree—over there! What a great plan.

We ignore problems because we are naive and codependent, but also because (3) we see ourselves as victims. Who got me on this slope anyway? If they had listened to me and not made me do this, I wouldn't be in this mess now, sliding on two plastic boards across snow and ice at 11,200 feet with two poles much too thin to bear my weight on a slope with a pitch of 45 degrees! I am the victim and therefore have a right to ignore and avoid this situation because it is not my fault anyway. Better for me to crash and die and let others weep bitter tears of regret at my funeral than that I should learn how to turn, shift my weight, and ski the fall line. That will show them—all of them!

When I suggest that ignoring problems is not a good thing, I am not suggesting anything profoundly novel. You've heard this all before. So why am I saying it now?

For this reason: Ignoring problems is one of the most common reasons we take tumbles in life, and if we are going to learn how to fall and get up again, recognizing the danger of "ignoreance" is important. If I address the issues that are in my life, there is no reasonable assurance that I will not fail miserably. But there is some redemptive value in falling while attempting to get it right: lessons are learned, and you have done precisely what was necessary to do. Remember, some falls in life cannot be avoided. But when you fall doing what is right, it can scarcely be regarded as a failure. It is a fall; it is that which happens to one in the human experience and on the pathway to growth. Ignoring the problem results in unnecessary failure, the by-products of which are low self-esteem, the reinforcement of inadequacy, and a sense of hopelessness.

Death

I do not want to be unduly melodramatic here. It is incredibly difficult to face the fall line. There is a false sense of safety in staying away from it, turning away from it. Actually to face the fall line takes courage—and a willingness to die! I say that somewhat "tongue in cheek," but there is some truth to it. The way down seems so far, the distance seems so steep! To do what I must do requires a little death. Then I face it, make the turn, keep my body facing the fall line, confront the fear, and off I go!

This is what Jesus is getting at when he talks about new growth in the Gospel of John. "Unless a grain of wheat falls into the earth and dies, it remains just a single grain; but if it dies, it bears much fruit" (12:24). Notice the words "falls" and "dies." These two words often go together. Leo Tolstoy, in his story "The Death of Ivan Ilych," has his character in his last moments describe his death as a "falling": "The example of a stone falling downwards with increasing velocity entered his mind. Life, a series of increasing sufferings, flies further and further towards its end…He stared at the back of the sofa and waited—awaiting that dreadful fall and shock and destruction."[1]

An old Islamic hadith says "die before you die." St. Francis says in his famous prayer that in dying we are born to eternal life. Paul says, "I die daily." Jesus expresses it yet another way in the Gospel of Luke: "For those who want to save their life will lose it, and those who lose their life for my sake will save it" (9:24).

There's a story of a man who was out hiking in the mountains and took a tumble over a ledge that sent him spinning down a precipitous slope. In desperation he reached out to grab something—anything—and, to his surprise and delight, snagged a small bush growing out of the crevice of the rock. Looking down and seeing that his situation was precarious, he looked up and shouted for help. He was amazed when he heard a voice respond, saying, "I am here. What do you want?"

The man was glad the stranger had happened by but was nonetheless nonplussed. "What do you mean, what do I want? I want you to save me."

The voice said, "I can do that."

"Good! Good! What do I do next?"

"Let go of the bush."

The man was shocked. "Who are you, anyway?"

"I am God. Let go of the bush."

Instead, the man tightened his grip on the bush. "Well, God, you certainly have impressive credentials, but perhaps you are not fully aware of the situation here. I have just fallen over this cliff, and my only current salvation is this scrawny bush; but it, too, shall soon give out. I am in peril of becoming carrion for the vultures circling overhead. I am afraid letting go of the bush is precisely what I cannot do."

"Let go of the bush."

There was silence. "If I don't let go of the bush, are you going to turn it into a burning bush, like you did for Moses?"

"Let go of the bush."

Again there was silence. Finally, he shouted louder, "Is there anyone else up there?"

I've heard this story told several times and in a variety of ways. It usually is told to express the necessity of faith in one's daily walk with God. But it is less about faith than about dying. It would have taken a small death for that man to release his hold on the bush. He needed to lose his life to save it; to give it up in order to get it back.

The apostle Paul's spin on this principle is articulated in yet another way in his letter to the Galatians. Paul was addressing a group of Christians who were still trying to pry open the door of the kingdom by doing, doing, doing. Paul attempts to make them understand the principle of being, being, being. They apparently thought that by keeping, or attempting to keep, every iota of the law of Moses, they could merit a pass into heaven. Paul knows that this approach is doomed to failure. Paul argues that living comes by dying. Better to understand that we "have been crucified with Christ." He continues: "It is no longer I who live, but it is Christ who lives in me" (2:19, 20).

It is the ultimate paradox, therefore, that we who wish to live must first die to experience the kind of life we want. We want an intimate relationship with our spouse, but we are too proud to admit our wrongness and responsibility. Only when we "die" and say "I am wrong" does a spark of life return to the relationship. We want to be successful at our job or career, but only when we die a little and say, "You know, I need some help on this" do we transform what is sure to be a painful death into something beautifully alive. When we forgive, we are forgiven; when we serve others, we ourselves are served; when we give, we receive more than we gave; when we sacrifice, we save the very thing for which we are dying.

Unless the life we live has those elements in it that are worth dying for, what is the content of our lives? Have you no relationship for which you would say "no" to yourself? Have you no work for which you would gladly deny yourself some pleasure? Have you no goals for which you would not be willing to pay a price? There is nothing in life worth having and living for that comes without a price, and that price is death.

Camus makes this point in *The Myth of Sisphysus*. Life is worth living when one has something worth dying for.

Rebuilding the Walls

There was once a good-natured fellow who was in the wrong place at the wrong time. During a Middle East conflict, he was captured and taken as a prisoner of war to the land of his conquerors, a middle eastern principality complete with a monarchy. Because, however, of his standing in his homeland, his background, and education, he was able to ingratiate his way into the very court of the king, where he daily had access to the ear of the monarch. He worked in the royal wine cellars and was the one who personally brought the king the *vin du jour*—whatever the king wanted.

One day, he heard that the capital city in his homeland was falling into ruin, that it had become the laughingstock of the neighboring political entities. The ancient walls, so beloved and so important to the city's identity and safety, were in a heap of stones, and those who passed by them laughed in scorn. Our young man earnestly desired to return to his home and work in his city. His heart was broken. But how could he approach the king with such a request? The king would no doubt sentence him to death for even suggesting that the city, a natural enemy, be refortified, and that he, a captured and enslaved servant, should be the instrument of that restoration!

Nehemiah, for that was his name, struggled with his fear. He tried the strategy of "ignoreance." How relieved he would have been if someone else had rebuilt the walls! How thankful he would have been if his information turned out to be false. But this did not happen. He tried to avoid the fall line, but he came to the point where he literally cared less for his life than he did for the walls of his beloved city. He went in to the king and told him what was troubling him. To his surprise, not only did the king listen without anger but gave him permission and the resources he needed to get the job done.

The whole story is told in a wonderful account in the book of Nehemiah in the Hebrew Bible.

Devin Murphy is a kicking coach for the Miami Dolphins. The Dolphins, led by coach Jimmy Johnson, were the worst kicking team in the 1996–1997 season. Jimmy looked for someone who could get his kicking game on track. He chose Devin. "If Devin produces," he said in a recent interview, "Devin stays. If he doesn't, he goes. His situation is just like mine. I have to produce or I'm gone."

Devin has never kicked a football in his life and never will. The man is in a wheelchair suffering from cerebral palsy. But he is an acknowledged expert on kicking and had several coaching jobs on the collegiate level before accepting this one with the Miami Dolphins. Devin is living life on the fall line.

The greatest achievements in human history have been accomplished by people like Devin Murphy who face the fall line with courage and vision!

Volunteer to Die!

There is another distasteful element to this discussion, and that concerns the voluntary nature of embracing the cross, a symbol of death. There are many risks we face in life every day. This is not what I mean by facing the fall line. This is simply life. When Jesus calls us to bear the cross, he calls us to embrace something we can choose *not to embrace*. I do not need to work at the hospice; I do not need to forgive; I do not need to accommodate; I do not need to give the other person preference; I do not need to let the other guy cut in front of me on the freeway; I do not need to give of my time; I do not need to suffer: *I choose to!*

That is facing the fall line! When I choose suffering, I am truly casting myself like a grain of wheat into the ground; I am truly affirming my crucifixion with Christ; I am truly taking and bearing the cross—I am facing the fall line.

Losing a job, coping with a serious illness, dealing with a cantankerous relative are all serious issues, but they do not involve embracing the cross. They do involve learning to live and cope and get along, serious and troublesome lessons in anyone's estimation. But if these situations are *LIFE 101* (the title of Jon Peter's best-selling book), bearing the cross is LIFE 201, 301, or 401 (there is no postgraduate work in this life).

Facing the fall line involves dying. It is a choice. Paradox once again comes into view. If I choose not to face the fall line, I will inevitably crash and be nothing more than a mangled tangle of paraphernalia. If I do face the fall line, it will take a voluntary "fall" or "death." It is the last thing you really want to do. But if you do it, you live!

NOTE

[1] Leo Tolstoy, "The Death of Ivan Ilych," in *The Story and Its Writer*, ed. Ann Charters (Boston: Bedford Books, 1995), p. 1274.

9

We Have Falling Expectations

Charlie Brown, Linus, and Lucy are on their way to school. It's show-and-tell time. Lucy asks Linus if he has remembered to bring anything for show and tell.

"Yes," Linus answers, "I have a couple of things here to show the class." He then unfolds some papers. "These are copies I've been making of some of the Dead Sea Scrolls," he says. Holding them up for Charlie Brown and Lucy to inspect, he continues: "This is a duplicate of the scroll of Isaiah, chapters 38—40. It was made from 17 pieces of sheepskin and was found in a cave by Bedouin shepherds."

Pulling out another piece of paper he says, "Here I have made a copy of the earliest known fragment ever found. It's a portion of 1 Samuel 23:9–16. I'll try to explain to the class how these manuscripts have influenced modern scholarship."

Lucy responds, "How interesting, Linus," and she turns to Charlie Brown, who has a frustrated expression on his face, and asks, "Are you bringing something for show and tell, Charlie Brown?"

"Well," says a dejected Charlie Brown, "I had a little red fire engine here, but I think I'll just forget it."

Charlie Brown had a strong sense he was about to fall! When stacked up against the impressive display of knowledge and insight Linus was offering, his meager idea seeming pitifully inadequate.

Since falling is part of the human experience, it is not surprising that we expect to fall. The expectation that we are going to fall in life is a good thing because when it happens, it doesn't come as a complete shock. On the other hand, the very expectation that we are going to fall can itself be a source of failure.

This is not to say that any given spill is inevitable. When the Green Bay Packers take the field during an NFL season, they expect to win every game, and indeed, every game is winnable. That is why coaches are fond of saying in the pre-game interview, "We just gotta take it a game at a time."

Will an NFL team go undefeated for the entire season? Highly unlikely. The last time it happened, Richard Nixon was president, gasoline was 34 cents a gallon, and bell-bottom jeans were the rage (Miami Dolphins, 17–0, 1972). But every game is winnable!

I am going to fall anyway, so why try? Because in the effort to succeed you achieve more than you do without the effort. As Wayne Gretsky, perhaps the greatest hockey player to play the game, has said, "You miss 100 percent of the shots you don't take."

Falling is not necessarily about me; it's about life. Psychologist Bo Lozoff pointed out recently that the answer of pop psychology and the self-help gurus to the problem of failure and self-esteem is to shout at ourselves and have others shout at us that we are good, we are special, we are unique, and we are wonderful. Lozoff contrasts this idea with the emphasis in most world religions of "forgetting" ourselves. The answer, he says, should focus less on me, me, me, and more on ski, ski, ski. That is, the focus should be on the experience of life itself. When we move away from ourselves to view life in its extraordinary, multi-various dimensions, even the experience of falling has value.

Sometimes I feel that everything is stacked against me. Life is like that, isn't it? Some days are good; others are not so good. Some days you're a pigeon; some days you're a statue. In his letter to the Romans, Paul targets this problem: "If God is for us, who can be against us?" Many of us take the answer to Paul's question to be: "Nothing and no one!" This must be the rationale for the pre-game prayers asking God to be on the side of "our" football team or basketball team. If God is on our side, we'll win.

The truth is that anyone, everyone, and everything can be against us, and they frequently are! Our neighbors can be against us, our boss can be against us, as can our ex-spouse and our coworkers. A storm may put two feet of water in our basement; the children may get sick; the promotion may fall through; the stock market may collapse. The litany goes on and on.

Paul's meaning, however, is this: If God is for us, no one and nothing can *prevail* against us! This depends upon an important caveat in Paul's continuing message: All things work together for good to those who are called according to God's purpose (Romans 8:30). The adversities of life will not prevail against those who are doing what is right, against those who have lined themselves up with God's purpose, against those who have abandoned their own selfishness for a larger arena of service to others.

In such a scheme of things, there is no person whom God cannot use in this life. Our estimation of ourselves need not be overly inflated or modestly undervalued. We are important to God; we are vital to the physical, emotional, and spiritual well-being of others.

How can I be happy if I am falling all the time? The question assumes that you have an inalienable right to happiness. The New Testament appears to teach that virtue, not happiness, is the goal. Viktor Frankl argues, as we have already noted, that if we do the right thing, "happiness ensues." When happiness is the objective, it is as elusive as trying to catch a cloud in the sky. Conversely, when our suffering is the focus of self-absorbed attention, happiness is equally elusive.

Let's return to Paul, because here is a man who was never far from failure and suffering, yet never raises the issue of happiness. Take a look at his resume of suffering:

> Five times I received…the forty lashes minus one. Three times I was beaten with rods, once I was stoned, three times I was shipwrecked, I spent a night and a day in the open sea, I have been constantly on the move. I have been in danger from rivers, in danger from bandits, in danger from my own countrymen, in danger from Gentiles; in danger in the city, in danger in the country, in danger at sea; and in danger from false brothers. I

have labored and toiled and have often gone without sleep; I have known hunger and thirst and have often gone without food; I have been cold and naked. (2 Corinthians 11:24–27, NIV)

Paul then goes on to describe a particular suffering from which he asked God to exempt him: "Three times I pleaded with the Lord to take it away from me," he says (2 Corinthians 12:8, NIV). We don't know what problem he's talking about here, although scholars have suggested a variety of possibilities, including an eye affliction.

God, however, had other ideas for Paul, and happiness does not seem to have been one of them. God gave Paul strength sufficient for the needs, not happiness sufficient for his wants. Paul thought he couldn't be happy until this problem was removed from his life: "Get it out of here, Lord!" God said, "I'm going to help you not by taking you out of the problem or the problem out of you, but by giving you strength right in the middle of it!"

Paul's attitude changed immediately. Failure and suffering were seen in a new light. While Paul never expected to fail, he understood that in his weakness, a superior kind of strength could shine through that would otherwise be hidden from view. The beauty of the diamond is exposed by the cutting, chipping, and polishing of the stone. The brilliance of the pearl is revealed after the prying apart of the shell of the oyster. The block of marble becomes a *David* only after bearing the brunt of Michelangelo's chisel and hammer. "That is why," Paul exclaims, "I delight in weakness, in insults, in hardships, in persecutions, in difficulties. For when I am weak, then I am strong" (2 Corinthians 12:10, NIV).

This is a difficult paradox: Your weakest moment is also the moment of your greatest strength! It is then that others see in you what they would never otherwise see: your grace, your strength, your courage, your faith—all qualities that they themselves desire to emulate and learn. Your life at the moment of your weakness becomes a pattern that others can model. You wield your greatest power not by getting out your cell phone, sending a fax, issuing directives by E-mail, but by modeling the persuasive power of a life of inner depth and character.

Paul here turns the concept of falling on its head. By transforming the falling experience into something positive, the suffering moment has ceased to be a "fall" and has instead become a moment of triumph!

10

We Have Falling Phobia

"Savor fear," says Kersek (Joe Don Baker), the private eye in the 1991 movie *Cape Fear* starring Jessica Lange, Nick Nolte, and Robert de Niro. Kersek and Sam Bowden (Nick Nolte) are hunkered down in the Bowden house waiting for Max Cady (Robert de Niro), the villain from hell, to break in.

Cape Fear is a raging moral preachment on the murky interplay between good and evil. The evil is as easy to spot as the negative/positive images that periodically punctuate the sequences. The first image of evil is (as it is so often) a cross, this time tattooed on the back of an ex-con. Hanging from the patibulum are the scales of justice and truth. Max Cady's taut and well-trained body reads like the King James Bible: *Vengeance is mine, saith the Lord; the Lord is my Avenger; the time is at hand.* When Cady is subjected to a strip search, the town cop (the late Robert Mitchum) says he doesn't know whether to look at him or read him.

The object of Max Cady's wrath is Sam Bowden, the lawyer who defended him on a rape charge fourteen years earlier. Sam, who spotted the villainy in Cady, buried a report on the rape victim's prior sexual history (which was then admissible in court). Had the report been introduced as evidence, Max surely would have been released and back on the streets—precisely where Sam knew he did not belong.

Max is out of prison now—a changed man. "I've discovered the feminine side of myself," he explains to Sam. That's not all. Entering prison illiterate, he emerges from prison literate and something of a genius in the fashion of a Hannibal Lector, the cannibalistic savant of *Silence of the Lambs*. Cady has studied law ("We're just two lawyers now talking shop," Sam hears him say), read the transcripts of his trial, and, sandwiched between these lawyerly pursuits, has somehow managed to read Nietzsche, Henry Miller, Thomas Wolfe, and various seventeenth-century philosophers.

The Fear of Loss

The reason I am sharing so much of this film with you is because of what Robert De Niro's character says about evil. It relates to why we dread falling, why we fear taking a physical, moral, financial spill. The evil mediated to the viewer of this film through the character of Max Cady and the evil that we are to fear is the *evil of loss*. "I'm going to teach you about loss," Cady mutters to Sam. Max understands the evil of loss. He lost his freedom, his family, a wife, children, and respect. He has returned to New Essex, he tells Sam, to be his salvation, to lead him through hell to paradise—to teach him about loss. And no one can do this better than Max Cady. "I am like God and God is like me."

Max the sociopath soon has Sam the lawyer reading the Bible—the book of Job. Perhaps there is no biblical figure so acquainted with what it meant to "fall" than Job. Sam learns about a godly man whose faith was severely tested by being required to experience loss: the loss of wife and children, the loss of house, flocks, and wealth, and almost the loss of faith. This gives Sam pause. Goodness and evilness are matters of degree. He is not the evil man Max Cady is, but he is not the good man Job was. Sam's infidelities have forced the family to flee to New Essex for a fresh start. He is still carrying on with female law clerks. He and his wife Leigh (Jessica Lange) have a tenuous relationship in which both are clinging to the wreckage of what they still hope they can call a marriage.

The one person other than Max who really understands the nature of evil as loss is Leigh Bowden. In a tearful plea near the end, she begs Cady to leave her daughter, Danielle, alone. She argues that she really does understand loss; she understands the suffering, the loss of time, the loss of years, the loss of companionship. She has felt it, knows it, and understands it. It is a connection that the two of them share, a connection he does not share with Danielle and for which reason he should not touch Danielle.

In the end, it is Max Cady who is bound for the promised land speaking in tongues and Sam Bowden who, pulling himself out of the waters of Cape Fear, discovers to his horror that there is blood on his hands.

Sam Bowden does not lose what he feared he might. Nevertheless, we are afraid of falling for this very reason: To fall is to lose something, and we can never be sure how deep the loss will be.

Life Wish

It is comforting to understand, however, that fear is common to us all. To be alive is to have experienced fear at some time. Indeed, the desire to experience fear in order to experience life explains certain behaviors many of us find bizarre. Like jumping out of an airplane with a parachute on. Why would any rational person want to do that? Or jumping off a bridge with a rubber band around the waist? Or hang gliding off the top of El Capitan in Yosemite? We say that people who do things like this have a death wish. In reality, they have a "life wish." They know that in the adrenaline rush, the increased heart rate, the furious flow of oxygen to the brain, the whoosh of air into the lungs— they truly "feel alive!"

Mabel Crider is a white-haired, sixty-year-old, married woman, with two adult children and two grandchildren, who by all accounts should be renewing her membership with AARP and soaking her feet in epsom salts. Instead, on her sixtieth birthday she skydives for the first time. Hadn't done it before; hasn't done it since. "Don't need to," she says. Now, what sort of foolishness would get into this grandma and cause her to strap on a parachute and jump out of a plane? Simple. She's got a life wish, that's all. (Incidentally, Mabel's mother-in-law lives with her and her husband; Helen's 101 and still driving!)

Another friend of mine, Craig Jeter, 35, did the same thing: jumped out of a plane from 10,000 feet up. Craig, however, is a quadriplegic. He jumped with someone and made a perfect landing. It was filmed by a local television crew. He didn't tell his mother what he was doing until it was over. Craig has a "life wish."

Phobic About Failure

So common is fear that particular fears develop into phobias and anxiety disorders that can severely and profoundly affect a person's life. Phobias are irrational fears that persist in spite of contravening evidence and are so strong that people will do almost anything to avoid the object or situation that causes it. Well-known phobias include agoraphobia, anachro-phobia, acrophobia, xenophobia, claustrophobia, etc. Some lesser-known phobias are:

Vegaphobia: fear of green foods
Boringphobia: fear of sermons
Nerdaphobia: fear of pocket protectors

What do you call a person who is phobic about failure? A man! It's part of the cultural burden of being what Eugene Wilson, professor of English at the University of Dayton, calls a "success object." Women may be objectified in terms of sex, but men, he argues, bear a similar objectification in terms of success. Men hate to fail. Men hate to lose. Men hate to be beaten across the intersection when the light turns green. Men hate to be cut off in traffic. Men hate to be beaten at racquetball. Men have a need to succeed. They're phobic about failure.

Not that women love to fail! But they tend to fear relationship failures and social rejection rather than professional failure. In both cases, the fear is a fear of loss: the loss of public approbation, the loss of friendship, the loss of security, the loss of income, and so on.

Fear Fallout

The fear of falling (or failure) may be a healthy thing, as we have already noted. But the first fallout factor of the fear of failure is that such a fear may cause the very thing feared! We call this the "self-fulfilling prophecy" syndrome, which is another way of paraphrasing Heraclitus, who said, "Character is destiny." Expectations create reality. What we fear will happen—that is, predict will happen—does in fact happen! Some people go so far as to argue that if something bad happens, we actually wished it to happen.

In the summer of 1997, Frank Rupp, 67, and his wife Rita, 57, decided to travel from their home in Tulsa, Oklahoma, to New York for a wedding. After the wedding, they would sightsee in New England. Then Frank would fly home to get back to the business, while Rita would drive the car back at her own pace.

Rita evidently did not fully share with Frank her fears about driving alone from New England to Tulsa. She also did not tell him that she wrote a little note that she kept hidden in her purse in case something went wrong. The note read: "Help! Kidnapped. Call Highway Patrol." She included two Oklahoma phone numbers and on the other side of the paper she wrote, "My Ford van, cream and blue Okla." Thus prepared, she and Frank attended the wedding in New York and then began their sightseeing trip through New England.

They stopped at a store to buy a travel iron, and after they left, a store employee found a twenty-dollar bill on the floor of the rest room. Tucked inside very neatly was Rita's note, which had fallen from her purse. This discovery launched a 24-hour interstate police manhunt that was covered by national television and newspaper outlets and that ended only after Frank happened to call Oklahoma to check on business at the office. "I'm sitting here enjoying a view of the ocean," he told his office manager, Brenda Ward. She said, "You have no idea what's going on, do you?"

Human fear can do that. It can leave everyone clueless. It paralyzes us when we attempt to achieve our goals. We fear the failure, we fear the past, we fear the future, we fear fear.

The second fallout factor is that the emotion of fear may cause people to reject arguments that are in their own best interests. If you have been given a ticket for speeding, you may end up in traffic school. There the instructor will flash slides of horrible accidents and injuries that have occurred because of speeding. You are supposed to leave a changed person. You will never speed again. Children are likewise exposed to the horrific dangers of drugs and smoking. They are shown graphic pictures of diseased lungs; they listen to adults wheezing on oxygen and debilitated by emphysema. Yet, incredibly, research shows that their behavior in these cases is little affected by such scare tactics. What works better is *slight* exposure to the dangers and information about what can be done about it. When high levels of fear are injected into the discussion, people shift into denial; the person thinks, "Oh well, I've already started smoking. I'm dead anyway; there's no point in stopping now."

A third fallout factor is total paralysis. The "deer in the headlights" syndrome roots our feet to the pavement in the face of an oncoming truck. We cannot move. We cannot make a change in the relationship, we cannot leave our job, we cannot confront the aggressive coworker, we cannot discipline our child, we cannot resist abusive behavior, we cannot challenge the in-laws.

Worry and Fear

Worry is the nagging suspicion that our fears may be true. The word itself comes from an old English word meaning "to choke or strangle." This is precisely the effect of worry in our lives.

Worry is extremely difficult to get rid of. It clings to you like a piece of static cellophane. Moreover, it is futile to tell a worrier to stop worrying. On the face of it, worrying is an energy-consuming, silly emotion. If something can be done about the object of our worry, then we should do it and stop worrying. If nothing can be done, then of what use is worrying? None at all. Yet, people who tell others to stop worrying and who try to show others the futility of worry fail to recognize that worry, as a small subset of fear, is not amenable to reason. It is an emotion that is triggered, like all emotions, by some external stimulus; it cannot be simply generated and likewise cannot be summarily dismissed.

WORRY

- God is our help in trouble; if you worry, you're on your own.
- Worry pulls tomorrow's cloud over today's sunshine.
- Worry is the interest paid on trouble before it's due.
- Worry is wasting today's time to clutter up tomorrow's opportunities with yesterday's troubles.

This view runs counter to conventional wisdom popularized by the Lion King approach to worry: Hakuna Matata. The whole thing is cute but in real life not really helpful.

Psychologist William James said that the essence of genius is knowing what to overlook. Worriers are phobically challenged persons incapable of overlooking anything. They fuss about incredible and often highly inventive possible scenarios. The only insight that I have found to be helpful to people who worry (inveterate, pathological worriers are beyond insight) is the notion that worry is connected with a concept of the future. We worry because we are aware of future consequences. Take away the future, and worry disappears. You are building a house. Rain delays the foundation work. You worry that the construction "will not be finished on time." That specific worry is tied directly to the idea of the future four months hence. You want to be in the house by Christmas. Take away Christmas, and worry vanishes.

To banish the invasive presence of the future requires aggressive attention to the present moment. Jesus said, "Do not worry about tomorrow, for tomorrow will bring worries of its own" (Matthew 6:34). He is not suggesting that planning and preparation are spiritually debilitating exercises. Rather, he is emphasizing that one's focus must be in space and time, not in a time warp where we have no control or input. Indeed, planning for the future is an activity done in the present, and it is the opposite of worry. Planning is a careful process of constructing a possible future; worry is a haphazard process of deconstructing an implausible future.

Overcoming Fear

What can we do about falling phobia? First, we can, as Susan Jeffers has suggested, feel the fear and do it anyway. When we learn to live with fear, we get that edgy feeling that suggests we have extended ourselves to the outer limits of our abilities, that we are testing the depth of our character, the extent of our competence. Failure, should it happen, then simply provides an edge, a boundary that marks off the territory of competence or the range of our abilities. We then live within that range, exploring it, coming to know it (ourselves) intimately, until we grow restless and are eager to explore beyond the boundaries again. When this happens, the fear returns like a small cramp in the stomach. You can feel its presence, but it is not strong enough to bend you over in numbing pain. You know you have extended yourself to the edge of fear.

Second, make friends of fear. Indeed, when we understand the positive role fear plays in our life we can overcome its negative influence. Fear can then become a friend. Pema Chodron, author of *When Things Fall Apart*, even suggests that "the next time you encounter fear, consider yourself lucky." Fear warns you of outright danger, it alerts you that you are sailing on the edge of your world, it confirms that you are perilously alive and determined to avoid "dying before you live." Therefore, fear can become a sort of intimate companion, a familiar emotion that, when it visits us, can be expected to benevolently guide us to where we need to go. "What we're talking about," writes Chodron, "is getting to know fear, becoming familiar with fear, looking it right in the eye....The truth is that when we really begin to do this, we're going to be continually humbled. There's not going to be much room for the arrogance that holding on to ideals brings."[1]

Third, discuss your fears, worries, and anxieties. Identify them. Trace them to their source. Develop possible strategies to minimize them.

Fourth, bring faith to your fears. Generation X says, "No fear." The trans-generation X, the Christ, also says, "No fear...for I have overcome the world." In other places we are invited to approach God concerning all of our anxieties and to open our lives to the irrational and unexpected peace that God offers to people with faith in their fear. "The peace of God...will guard your hearts and your minds in Christ Jesus" (Philippians 4:7). The word "guard" evokes the image of a military garrison. God's peace stands at guard to keep marauding fears at bay.

Finally, bring passion to your fears. The scriptures remind us that "perfect love casts out fear" (1 John 4:18). If your child is menaced by a stranger, there is no amount of fear that can, in that moment, overpower your passion, your love for your child, your anger toward the aggressor, your incredible drive to protect your loved one. Developing a passionate lifestyle pushes fear into the shadows and corners of your life, removes it not altogether from your existence, but to a respectable distance where its presence can be felt only when necessary.

A good friend who is well known in the community where I live for his wry humor, his self-effacing private manner, and forceful public manner confessed recently that speaking in public, whether to make an announcement or give a report, is a very difficult chore. His throat tightens up, his knees weaken, his respiratory system goes into overdrive. He feels that his entire body is on the verge of total meltdown. Those of us who listened to this confession were amazed because, not knowing his private fear and only his public persona, we could not believe that such a self-assured person could be afflicted with this kind of terror.

How did my friend Darren shake this monkey off his back? It took courage, no doubt. But his courage was born of a deeper passion to experience and experiment, to risk and to recover, to try and err if necessary. It is this passion for life that defines the Darren that I know and that consequently masks the fear he sometimes feels as he approaches certain responsibilities for which he feels he has little natural aptitude. Love perhaps does not "cast out" fear, for the fear is still there. But love is always able to conquer fear.

Darren himself knows of an acquaintance in the east who recently lost a leg in a farming accident. When the doctor was fitting him for a prosthesis the patient refused to take some practice falls. He would not fall! The doctor told him that unless he was willing to fall, the doctor would not fit him with a prosthesis that would enable him to walk. The patient declined and is in a wheelchair to this day. The accident claimed not only a leg, but a heart; the victim lost not only a part of his body, but a chunk of his spirit as well.

The mantra of Generation X is "No fear" and in the *fin de siecle* postmodern malaise, Xers argue that there is little left to fear. Boomer parents worry about their Buster children because they know a little fear is healthy medicine. The Old Testament sage observed, "The fear of the Lord is the beginning of wisdom." It is an aphorism that can easily be adapted to other contexts: I make backup copies of my disks. This is a very wise thing to do. Sometimes vacuuming the family room is also very wise.

But if the beginning of wisdom is fear, it is only the beginning. Fear may give birth to wisdom, but wisdom quickly grows up, leaving fear and generating behaviors and attitudes that have little to do with fear. The question that should be addressed concerning our fears is: What does this fear have to teach me? When that can be answered, the way has been prepared for the fear to be left behind.

What we are talking about here, however, is not the kind of fear that generates wisdom. That's GoodFear. We should all have it, or at least begin with it. There is another kind of fear: BadFear, that generates not wisdom but foolishness. Phobias fall into this category, but other fears fit as well: fear that the spouse will leave, fear that the job is not secure, fear of the future, fear of trusting, fear of commitment. Yet, even these fears are not invincible. It is not something with which we always need to live. Darren's fear of speaking is still with him, but he has learned that he can control the fear. The fear is dead, but Darren is treating it as though it lives. It still has the power to frighten him, although not control him. It is a sort of vampire emotion, an UnFear, a fear that is dead but comes alive at inopportune moments to frighten and thrill. So far, Darren has been pulling out garlic and crucifixes to control the beast. Someday, he'll grab a stake and drive it through its heart.

The name of the stake is love. "Savor fear," says Kersek. Yes, savor it, because the taste of fear is a prequel to the taste of an even more powerful emotion that will vanquish it: the power of love!

NOTE

[1]Pema Chodron, "Making Friends With Fear," *The Utne Reader*, May-June, 1997, pp. 63-66 in passim.

11

We Have Falling Folly

Falling is often nothing more than sheer stupidity. I know that's a strong word, but it's true. It's also a word that is being used frequently to describe our behavior. Radio talk show call-in host and psychologist Dr. Laura Schlessinger recognizes that sometimes we do stupid things that work against us. Her book *Ten Stupid Things Women Do to Mess Up Their Lives* addresses behavior patterns that women sometimes fall into that complicate rather than simplify their lives. Among such traps are Stupid Attachment, Stupid Passion, and Stupid Expectations. A book could be, and probably will be, written about the stupid things men do. Stupidity is not a gender-specific syndrome; we all do stupid things and say stupid things at some point in our lives. President Bush once said, "Some reporters said I don't have any vision. I don't see that." Someone wrote this line in the 1992 Nissan owner's manual: "Make sure your hands are inside before closing the window." When once asked if he had made up his mind, Yogi Berra said, "Not that I know of."[1]

Stupidness has become a growth industry. Hollywood produces "Dumb and Dumber." The movie grosses millions. Dan Butler is the creator of the "America's Dumbest Criminals" books and TV series. His favorite story is of the guy who went into a store and asked for change

70

for a twenty. When the clerk opened the cash register, he demanded all the money. There was only about $8 in the till, and he left his $20 there. So the guy lost $12 on the robbery."

Then there is the thief who wanted to rob a jewelry store. He picked up a brick and threw it at the window—not realizing that the window was made of plexiglass. It hit the window with a thud, bounced back, and hit the erstwhile robber on the head, knocking him out cold. He was still unconscious when police arrived on the scene.

Chuck Shepherd's book *America's Least Competent Criminals* tells of bank robbers who fled to a McDonalds hoping to blend with the crowd. The police managed to spot them among about thirty suburbanites because they were the ones with the tattoos—and the wads of cash bulging out of their socks.

Thieves haplessly announce their identities with amusing consistency. One guy wore a work shirt to his robbery—with his name over one pocket. Another covered the license plate on the getaway car but kept the "for sale" sign. Cops later called the phone number and asked if the owner had a van for sale. The guy said sure and provided his address—to which the police went and arrested the man without incident.

So what do *we* do that is so stupid when it comes to skiing the slopes of life? Here's the list:

Stupid Thing Number 7: We Don't Take Instruction

Why is it that we have such a hard time asking for help? Men particularly seem to find this difficult. What can be so hard about strapping on skis, keeping your knees bent and feet together, and steering yourself down this little hill? And we've even got these handy little poles in each hand to prop us up. No problem. I'll be fine.

Why is it that it is so hard for us to go to counselors or therapists to get help for ourselves or a relationship? Why won't we admit our neediness? Why is vulnerability such a liability for a male in our culture?

You know the answer. It has to do with the need to be in control, associating vulnerability with weakness, yada yada yada.

Listen, guys. Let me tell you something: There's no way you or anyone else is going to get down this mountain we call life without hellacious, bodacious, and audacious crashes along the way, unless you get some help and instruction and take a few lessons, and you'd best admit it now and save yourself and your loved ones a lot of grief and pain. You know what I mean? Is there anything in this paragraph you don't understand?

Stupid Thing Number 6: We Ignore Bad Weather

When you want to do something badly enough, even the prospect of bad weather won't keep you from doing it. Nimbus-cumulus thunderclouds are stacking up in the sky, lightning bolts are dancing in the air, pellets of rain are tattooing your face, but you persist. And then you are in the thick of it.

You want to have a serious discussion with your spouse about changing the wallpaper in the bathroom? Don't do this within a 24-hour period in which she has just hung new wallpaper in the bathroom. You want to tell your spouse about your day at work? Don't do this while he is attempting to watch Jocko give the sports report on Channel 9. You want to borrow some money without your spouse knowing? In the first place, never do this, because your spouse will always, always find out. In the second place, don't borrow money from Manny, who operates out of the trunk of his 1956 DeSoto, even if he has a Collector license plate wired to the fender. Don't drive the car on bald tires thinking you can squeeze another thousand miles out of them. Don't loan money to your sister-in-law expecting that you'll ever see the money again. Don't marry the bum who has an 8 a.m. tee time on the day you're getting married at noon.

Can you see the problems here? Sometimes the conditions are not right to do what you want to do. It is better to experience the inconvenience of delay than the inconvenience of disaster.

Stupid Thing Number 5: We Use Poor Equipment

We don't check the equipment. The skis have not been waxed, the edges are rough, the bindings are falling apart, and the boots don't fit right. Then we wonder why we fall!

Relationships are high maintenance. Life is high maintenance! Life does not happen well without attention to the details. Someone has said, "God is in the details." Someone needs to be in the details, but God isn't in the details you've overlooked or that belong to you. God is in God's own details; you have to tend to your own. God isn't going to take your wife out to dinner Friday night. God isn't going to put a new set of tires on the car. God isn't going to get a Super Channel Surf remote control for your husband. God isn't going to spend time with your kid. God isn't going to write that paper. God isn't going to draft that report.

God will be in the details when you pay attention to the details.

Stupid Thing Number 4: The Need for Speed

We are tempted to go too fast. The way ahead is often deceptively easy. Soon things are out of control.

American culture is notorious for its fast-paced lifestyle. We have a difficult time with the concept of waiting. We run red lights to avoid sitting at an intersection for 30–45 seconds. We chafe with irritation as we stand in line waiting for the next bank teller. We resent sitting in the doctor's office waiting for the doctor to catch up on his or her schedule. We dart in and out of traffic to get ahead but usually end up at the stoplight side by side with the slow-moving car we passed a few minutes before.

The frenetic lifestyle contributes to this sense of urgency and a skewed understanding of what it means to be "productive." With laptop computers, faxes, and cell phones, one need never leave the office. It can go wherever you go. Author Noelle Oxenhandler, in her essay "Fall From Grace," makes this very point:

> But here is the lawyer, riding the train between Tarrytown, where he lives, and New York City, where he works. It's a beautiful ride, along the Hudson River, past the Tappan Zee Bridge and the high green cliffs of the Palisades. He could spend the early-morning commute watching the slowly emerging sun break the dark river into moving strokes of gold and pink light. But all the while he is calling, tapping, speaking to people who are somewhere else....Everything can come with him now, onto the train. Every moment can be maximally productive.[2]

If we speed to work, we also speed into debt. We hardly think twice about running up credit card debt in order to get now what we could get later for cash. Credit card issuers mailed out 2.1 billion solicitations in 1994, enough for eight cards for every American. Americans are staggering under the weight of nearly $1 trillion in installment loans—almost twice the level of ten years ago. The average household carries $3,900 in credit card debt.

We don't know what it means to slow down. Writer Kiran Desai addresses this theme in his story "The Sermon in the Guava Tree." What's so wrong with doing nothing, he asks? No work, no career, no ambition—just full-time, luxuriant laziness.

Sampath, a usually responsible son, was one day discovered missing. His family found him sitting in a guava tree. Sampath watched his family below and thought, "I am happy here…I am adopting a simple way of life." Sampath's family could not persuade him to come down, so in desperation they visited the holy man who lived outside the tea stall near the deer park.

> "Sorry to disturb you. Our son is afflicted."
> "How is he afflicted?"
> "He is suffering from madness."
> "Is he shouting?"
> "No."
> "Having fits?"
> "No."
> "Is he tearing his hair out?"
> "No."
> "Is he biting his neighbors? Biting himself? Is he sleepwalking? Does he stick out his tongue and roll his eyes? Is he rude to strangers?"
> "No. He eats and sleeps and takes good care of his hair. He doesn't shout and he doesn't bite himself. He has never been rude to strangers."
> "Then he is not mad."
> "But he is sitting up in a tree!"
> "Arrange a marriage for him. Then you can rest in peace. You will have no further problems."[3]

Recently I was in New York City on business. Having a couple of hours free in the afternoon, I strolled up to Central Park and enjoyed a walk through playgrounds, woods, and fields. I could hear the jingle of the carousel not far away. I sat down on a park bench and watched the people passing by and a softball game in progress just a holler away. Suddenly, I "woke" with a start, looked at my watch, and realized that I had been sitting on that park bench for 45 minutes—doing nothing. Usually that is difficult for me. I smiled with satisfaction because I took it as a sign of moral development that I could spend 45 minutes in quietness without feeling guilt for not "doing" anything.

Stupid Thing Number 3: Hotdogging

It's easy to spot the hotdoggers on a ski slope. Everything they do calls attention to themselves. They race down easy slopes, whizzing by slower and less skilled skiers, frightening them, and sometimes causing them to lose control and fall. They ski to be seen and admired. They succeed at the former, fail miserably at the latter. No one likes hotdoggers.

Hotdoggers are highly skilled at what they do. These so-called type A personalities are successes at their careers, but failures at life. They are valued as professionals, but laughed at as persons. They sign big contracts, but can't keep little commitments. They are spirited, but not spiritual. They have it all, but still don't get it. They utterly fail to understand the people around them; they engender no respect from those with whom they work; they get little sympathy when they face reversals of fortune.

If you are interested in walking the broad pathway of worldly attention, then hotdogging is for you. If, however, you choose to walk the narrow, rugged pathway of virtue, the world will ignore you. But it is the narrow path that is the path of true success.

In 1997, after the infamous Tyson-Holyfield heavyweight fight, a reporter noted the lengths to which the media sought interviews from Mike Tyson and his promoter, Don King. He went on to contrast the media frenzy surrounding Tyson and King with the approach to Holyfield.

> In all honesty, no one would ride to the edge of the desert to talk with Evander Holyfield. No one much cared about Holyfield. He was likable enough. But he was dull copy. He hadn't raped anyone. He hadn't been to jail. He talked about Jesus Christ all the time and literally sang gospel music while hitting the heavy bag. He seemed like a good fellow, but what story did he offer? He talked in the polite clichés of doing my best, having faith in my abilities and in the will of God—but what did he mean? Heavyweight championship fights, from the days of John L. Sullivan onward, are stories, morality plays, and this story, regardless of its end, was all about Tyson.[4]

If Mike Tyson is the hotdogger, Evander Holyfield is the colddogger. The Bible is full of hotdoggers and colddoggers: Cain? Hotdogger. Abel? Colddogger. Saul, hotdogger; young David, colddogger (the older David frequently got into trouble hotdogging). Abraham, colddogger; Lot, hotdogger. Samson, hotdogger. Peter, hotdogger. Daniel, colddogger.

Hotdoggers are interesting and get a lot of press; colddoggers are boring, but have a lot of peace. Hotdoggers call attention to themselves for their own glory; colddoggers call themselves to attention to serve others. Hotdoggers value the destination; colddoggers cherish the journey; hotdoggers stress skills; colddoggers stress safety. Hotdoggers are aggressive; colddoggers are considerate.

God clearly calls us to be colddoggers.

Stupid Thing Number 2: We Don't Eat Right

Irina Petranovich of Russia has been in America for two years. Her English is thickly accented, but very good. She is working on a degree in English at Metropolitan State College in Denver. There is much she enjoys and appreciates about American culture, but she makes this interesting observation: "You get up early," she says, "and scramble to get to work, get the kids to school. You work hard all day and sometimes two jobs. And for what purpose? To rush home and watch TV! This I do not understand."

She is right. The average American watches over five hours of television every day. And, if it were not enough that our children are too often nurtured by the electronic babysitter, now electronic games have emerged as yet another mindless electronic activity neutralizing the brain cells of our children. Parents not only have their own spirituality to worry about, but that of their children as well.

In fact, just living one day in our culture saps our spiritual reserves. In a violent, materialistic, and competitive society, nurturing one's spirituality must be an intentional activity. If it is not, one's inner resources tumble like the seashore into an ocean of fatigue and ennui. Our souls are depleted daily and therefore require daily energizing.

My wife recently found a sourdough recipe from her grandmother and decided to create a "starter" batch of sourdough. From this starter, she made some bread, and from now on, whenever she needs dough, she can go to the refrigerator and get what she needs for the day. The critical element of this process, however, is that when she takes something from the sourdough mix, she must add some flour and milk to keep the mixture active. Her grandmother used the sourdough mix every day for years. There are some cases in which a mother has given starter dough to married daughters and they to their daughters so that the dough lives somehow in perpetuity!

The point is that we must add to the mixture, or it runs dry and runs out. Just living in the world exhausts our spiritual reserves; we must add nourishment to the mix daily to prevent energy depletion.

What type of nourishment do we need, and where can we get it? Television is not an option for nourishment. There is good programming on television, but even watching good programs is the electronic equivalent of fast food. It is a passive form of nourishment that may have residual benefits from the mere opportunity to sit down and relax. Some mind training may take place. But that's about it.

The body. Attention must first be given to the physical body. When we eat right and exercise properly, the body not only feels better, but that healthy feeling is good for our souls. Proper care of the body is a soul issue. If you don't believe me, just recall the last time your body was ill from an infection or disease. How perky did you feel in your soul during this time? Most of us are not able to transcend the needs of the body, to be unaffected in our souls. What happens to the body affects us spiritually. Therefore, soul care begins with the body.

The mind. Next, we can give attention to our minds. The training of our minds enables us to channel life-giving energy to our souls. If you have no training in art appreciation, art will not provide renewal for your soul as richly as it does for those who have studied art. If you have no training in music, you are shut off to a significant degree to the curative power of music in your life. If you have no interest in good literature, you shut yourself off from the wisdom of others. If you do not study the scriptures, you cannot tap into the written and revealed word of God as a source of strength and inspiration.

My point here is not to denigrate those who have no interest in art, music and Bible study. Many people find renewal in activities that do not engage the mind, such as fishing, golf, hiking, working on an old car, gardening, and so on. All of these endeavors have value, and I do not discount them. But it is also true that, all other things being equal, the person who has taken the time to train the mind opens himself or herself up to worlds of renewal that were hitherto not possible.

The soul. How then can we feed the soul? Feed and exercise your body. Feed and exercise your mind. Then do three "soul" things: relax with God, relax with friends, and relax with yourself. In other words, pray, play, and get plenty of sleep.

Stupid Thing Number 1: We Go It Alone

Solitude can be a good thing; loneliness is debilitating. No man is an island. So said the poet. Henry David Thoreau observed that the mass of men "lead lives of quiet desperation." One of the lessons of the Adam and Eve story is that human beings fundamentally need each other. We are not made to survive alone.

Every rule of safety instructs us to be with someone. Don't climb mountains alone. Don't ski alone. Don't go swimming alone. Don't walk through the park alone. Don't jog alone.

The best insurance against falling is to be in the presence of those whose strength can hold us and whose very presence in our lives is an encouragement. The mantra of sci-fi afficionados is at least in part correct: "We are not alone." Or, we certainly do not need to be alone.

The positive results of being in company with those who can share your concerns and provide support is that together you create an experience more beautiful than you might have known separately. Occasionally, this means letting someone else get the credit, someone else receive the glory. Your role sometimes will be to be the "wind beneath the wings" while someone else soars.

A conductor of one of America's leading symphony orchestras was asked recently to name the instrument he thought was the most difficult to play. After thinking the question over for a moment, he replied, "Second fiddle. I can get plenty of first violinists. But to find one who can play second fiddle with enthusiasm is often a problem. If we have no second fiddles, we have no harmony."

There can be no harmony when we go it alone.

NOTES

[1]Ross Petras and Kathryn Petras, *The 776 Even Stupider Things Ever Said* (New York: HarperCollins, 1994).

[2]Noelle Oxenhandler, "Fall From Grace," *The New Yorker*, June 16, 1997, p. 65.

[3]Kiran Desai, "The Sermon in the Guava Tree," *The New Yorker*, June 23, 1997, p. 90f.

[4]David Remnick, "Kid Dynamite Blows Up," *The New Yorker*, July 14, 1997, p. 48.

III

How to Fall without Breaking Something Important

12

Grab a Parachute!

The kindly rain doth fall upon
The just and unjust fella,
But mostly on the just, because
The unjust stole the just's umbrella.

—Leo Rosten

Unlike myself, many people enjoy the emotion of falling. They jump from airplanes, hot air balloons, bridges, skyscrapers, and high mountain cliffs. They dive off thirty-meter platforms and oceanside bluffs. They strap themselves into harnesses attached to taut rubber cords at the amusement park and are sprung high into the air to bounce around in a death-defying dance of craziness.

When they pull stunts like this, however, they don't do it without elaborate protection. They realize that there are some very important body parts that can be injured in a fall, that, in fact, their very lives are at risk. Similariy, we also put at risk some very important spiritual body parts as we travel through life. Sometimes we actually suffer breaks— breaks in a marriage, job, career, trust, self-esteem, reputation, and financial security. Occasionally, the fall results in the death of the marriage,

81

the death of a career, or the death of trust. Therefore, those who are planning to fall because they think it's fun prepare diligently! They test the winds, check and double-check the equipment, attend classes, read books, watch videos, talk to others who have done what they propose to do, and work out to get into optimum physical shape.

The Free Fall

People, if they are going to fall, prefer different styles. Some prefer to free-fall. They enjoy falling without restraints: wild, explosive, creative, spectacular. This is the kind of fall that one doesn't plan for. It's the type of experience you think will never happen to you, and then it happens to you.

Perhaps you are the type who lives life in such a careless manner that all of your falls are crazy, out-of-control experiences that leave you dazed and your head spinning. But you prefer to free-fall, and you create a free-for-all in the lives of everyone around you. You're highly creative, but some see you as irresponsible. You have a zest for life, but the preoccupation with extreme skiing results in a lot of time in the snow bank or the hospital. Others continue to ski past you in a steady course toward their destination.

Still, the free fall can happen to any of us without warning. This very week, as I write this, two friends were killed in a car accident. She was driving, had a heart attack, and was dead before the car left the pavement. Their three adult children are now suddenly without parents; their grandchildren are without grandparents. In another year when the children look back on this week, it will all be a blur to them. Why? Because they are free-falling. Events beyond their control are pushing, shoving, and leading them. There are papers to sign, arrangements to be made, people to see. They move from one thing to the next, struggling only to keep up. That is why so often after a tragic event such as this, when the free fall is over and the affected party is once again emotionally conscious, the harsh and horrible reality sets it. This is the period of the greatest pain, yet it is a time when the victims are most overlooked.

The Controlled Fall

Others, not preferring to free-fall, try to control the fall. The fall itself may be unexpected, but they are prepared to act once it happens.

Mountain climbers are taught how to fall when traversing steep snow fields. If you fall and find yourself hurtling down the slope knowing that within seconds you will crash on the rocks below, you are to roll over so that you are face down as you fall. The point of the head of the ice axe is slowly thrust deeper and deeper into the snow, cutting a gash in the snow as you fall downward. It doesn't take long until the drag of the ice axe in the snow arrests your fall. You have fallen, but you have controlled the fall and the damage.

People who prefer a controlled fall are savers and planners and worriers. They always have Plan B in case Plan A goes wrong. Usually there is also a Plan C.

The Proactive Fall

Have you ever known without a doubt that you were going to fall moments before it happened? This fall announces its own arrival. You can see it coming. Since the fall is inevitable and if you wait for it to happen to you something might be seriously damaged, you elect to initiate the fall yourself and thereby minimize the damage.

You are skiing fast, perhaps too fast. You see a tree looming large in your direct line of vision. You know what is going to happen. Therefore, before it does, you take a crash into the snow.

Bret Favre, quarterback for the Green Bay Packers, drops back for a pass. Then he sees an opening and starts to run for yardage. A defensive linebacker shows up fifteen yards downfield. Favre knows what is going to happen. He runs as far as he can, and then he tumbles to the field before anyone can lay a hand on him. He takes the proactive fall.

I was rollerblading around a lake near where we live. Up ahead on the cement track around the lake was a family with three small children. I slowed down as I approached them. When I was about twenty feet away, one of the children moved directly into my path. I knew I could not stop in time, and in order to avoid her, I swerved to the side,. When I saw that I was going to go off the track, however, I decided that since I was going to fall, I would fall on my own terms. I sort of gave myself a push and a jump, landed on my side, and rolled a couple of times. No damage done.

People who take the proactive fall are skilled at discerning flaws and problems where others cannot see them. They invest time and energy into learning as much as they can about the experience. They try to get as much as they can out of it. When they bounce back, they are eager to give it another go, convinced they'll go farther next time.

The Parachute

It helps to have a parachute. This parachute has three ropes: aptitude, attitude, and altitude. Develop an aptitude, get an attitude, and rise to some altitude.

Aptitude. We have already established that, as human beings, we all have an unfortunate aptitude for falling. It happens all the time. We do not necessarily have an aptitude for doing it well. But aptitude can be developed.

It's hard to express what aptitude is, but we know it when we see it. When we observe a child attempting to build a house of plastic blocks, even if she fails, we can see that she has the aptitude for it, and someday she'll get it and clap her hands for joy. Aptitude, then, is a person's ability to acquire skills or knowledge in the future. Achievement, on the other hand, is those skills that have been acquired, perhaps as a result of one's aptitude to acquire them.

A child, for example, has an aptitude for balance and, therefore, for riding a bike. Most children can and will ride a bike. Of course, we start them out on training wheels. After they have learned how to pedal to gain forward momentum and have become familiar with the sensation of movement, we remove the training wheels. Then the falling begins! Some are able to master it immediately, but most experience several falls. However, they get back on and soon, after we have released our hands from the seat, they are surging forward under their own power. Children have an aptitude to learn, experience, grow; and falling, failing, not getting it right the first time, are simply a part of their lives.

We could adopt the training-wheel approach to life and wobble through life with our side wheels spinning and there for protection. But to really enjoy the experience of life, we take those training wheels off. We get rid of the safety net, we abandon conditions and limits and what-ifs, and we go for it. And we fall.

But we have the aptitude! We shall go on to do great things!

Attitude. Get an attitude! Get a new attitude!

Get an attitude of gratitude. Alcoholics Anonymous stresses the importance of having an attitude of gratitude. Complaining takes a lot of energy; gratitude is natural and easy and wears so well on both you and those upon whom it is bestowed.

Get an attitude of patience. Neither you nor your colleagues and friends are finished products. We are dynamic personalities constantly changing and capable of incredible growth. Give yourself time to learn how to be human.

Get an attitude of tolerance. Why should we, who fall so often ourselves, be critical of others who stumble as we do? Do we judge others on the basis of external distinctions rather than internal and intrinsic qualities?

We will develop these attitudes and other Christ-like qualities if we perceive the payoff is right. We hold on to entrenched attitudes like life preservers because we think there is a cognitive, social, or psychological payoff. We cling to attitudes for which we have old information and stereotypes that support our attitudes. There seems to be no cognitive reason to change. We harbor old attitudes because we have the support of friends and family who believe as we do. Letting go of that attitude would be to break with the family structure and cast us in the role of an outsider. We hang on to negative attitudes because it allows us to feel superior to others and boosts our self-esteem.

Altitude. If you don't have enough altitude, grabbing a parachute isn't going to help much! It is important to gain altitude in life, rise above the battle, get beyond the irritations you have hitherto felt were so important.

Ray Bradbury argued that "if we listened to our intellect, we'd never have a love affair, we'd never have a friendship, we'd never go into business because we'd be so cynical." He went on to say, "That's nonsense. You've got to jump off cliffs all the time and build your wings on the way down."[1]

Make sure it's a high cliff.

NOTE

[1]Source untraced.

13

Forgive

"To err is human, to forgive divine."—the Bible

"Don't get mad; get even." —conventional wisdom

"Don't get even; get it all." —Ivana Trump

It is a mistake to believe that people want to be forgiven. You don't think so? How many times has someone, anyone—a spouse, close friend—come up to you and said, "Excuse me, but I have wronged you; please forgive me"? Who wants to be forgiven? To accept forgiveness is an admission of guilt, and admitting guilt in our litigious society, in these testosterone times, in this manic millennium, is a very uncool thing to do. Take a survey. How many people really like that prayer of confession on Sunday mornings? The truth be told, we're not too happy admitting we are in need of God's forgiveness. We're praying this prayer and thinking, "But what have I done?"

I suggest that you move slowly when you're thinking about going to a friend, coworker, or even your spouse and letting them in on your little secret. "Honey, I forgive you," you say.

She looks at you as though you've lost your mind and says, "You forgive *me*? Excuse me? Don't you *honey* me. *You're* the one who was out of control! *I'm* the one who should be forgiving *you*. And I'll tell you something else—I'm not going to; not now, not ever!"

There you have it! You can't just jump on someone about whom you have been harboring a grudge, get in their face, and say, "I forgive you." That sort of sanctimonious arrogance is likely to get you nothing but grief. Here are three things to remember:

- Forgiveness is not something you do for the other person; it is something you do for yourself.

- Forgiveness is less an action than an attitude.

- Forgiveness as an attitude must precede forgiveness as an action.

Jesus Is the Great Forgiver

It may come as a surprise that, although guys really trip over the words "I'm sorry," as a rule they love to forgive. The reason for this is that we're talkers. Deborah Tannen, author of *You Just Don't Understand!* and *Put Down That Paper and Talk to Me,* argues that study after study shows that men generally talk more in public settings than do women. Men love to show off in the public arena. This is where they can put their competence on display. This is where the power plays happen. Yet, the same guy who is talking all day at the office won't say ten words in the private domain at home.

Men are quite willing to say "I forgive you" because saying those words implies a position of moral superiority. I…forgive…you! I, as the wounded party, and possessed of clear moral vision, and having a generous spirit and a warm heart, forgive you, the one who has caused my pain; you, the one who is lower than a worm in a wagon rut; you, whom no other person on earth would be willing to forgive. I, out of the goodness of my good, morally pure heart…forgive…the vile little creature you are.

Now, that is exactly how it sounds to the person being "forgiven." This is not how to "do" forgiveness.

As humans, we always do better with a model to emulate. We need pictures, a map, or directions. God knew this; it explains the incarnation. God's entrance into human experience at Bethlehem is, in part, explained by the fact that humans need someone to show them how to do things. Jesus, indeed, not only spoke of forgiveness in his earthly ministry, he modeled it. The principle he left with us is articulated by Paul: "Just as the Lord has forgiven you, so you also must forgive" (Colossians 3:13).

How did Jesus do it? The answer is simple. When you're on a cross, there's not much you can *do*. At Golgotha, his hands are nailed to the patibulum; he cannot touch anyone, he cannot give something, he cannot even make a visible gesture of forgiveness. His feet, likewise, are anchored to the cross. Jesus can't go anywhere. He can't make a visit to the homes of his offenders. You can't "do" forgiveness from a cross.

Paul's words that "just as the Lord has forgiven" us, so we "also must forgive" applies to us because, as followers of Christ, we ourselves have voluntarily taken up the cross. Without living in the way of the cross, we cannot be true disciples of Christ. Getting in people's faces announcing their forgiveness is not the way of the cross. When someone is in need of your forgiveness, whether they realize it or not, to forgive the Jesus way is to remember that you're on a cross, and there isn't much for you to do, and the less you do, the better.

Forgiveness Is the Absence of Action

Forgiveness, then, is the absence of action.

- It is the absence of revenge.
- It is the absence of false piety.
- It is the absence of a sanctimonious, holier-than-thou spirituality.
- It is the absence of spiritual pretense.
- It is the absence of the assumption that you are the offended one and not the offender.
- It is the absence of the assumption that you can read the mind of your alleged tormentor.
- It is the absence of the assumption that you understand his or her intention and moral motivation.

Seventy-seven Times

This is the only way Jesus' statement about forgiving "seventy-seven times" makes any sense (Matthew 18:22). Jesus is suggesting here that there must be no limit to our forgiveness. What makes this such a hard saying is the notion that forgiveness is something we must *do* "seventy-seven times." Just thinking about it gives me a mental cramp. If I must forgive someone seventy-seven times, that is a sure indication that the offender "doesn't get it." The offender is obviously not mending his ways. But that's the point! Forgiveness is not about keeping score! It is not something we do for the other guy; it is something we do for ourselves. It is not an action, but an attitude!

When we understand that forgiveness is not about heroic deeds, but about a heroic attitude, what Jesus says makes perfect sense. You can count actions, but you don't count attitudes. Jesus doesn't keep a forgiveness score. There are no forgiveness bean counters in the kingdom of God.

Keeping Score

Men, especially, are into keeping score. It doesn't matter what it is—playing golf, how many hot dogs I can eat, who has the biggest piece of pie, who said grace last, whose turn it is to feed the baby—it doesn't matter. We love to keep score. That's why we are much more comfortable with a bean-counting conception of forgiveness. It's the next best thing to revenge. When I have been wronged, I can tell the dirtbag that I've forgiven him. That works for me!

But Jesus turns this upside down and says we must not *do* something, but *be* something! Doing nothing when we've been wronged is the hardest thing in the world for "keeping score" mentalities like mine. Everything in me, all that I am—cries out for action. In this, I am no different than the twelve disciples Jesus hung out with. They thought that raining down fire from heaven would be a good idea for the villages that did not accept them (Luke 9:54). Jesus said no. He also said to "rejoice and be glad" when "people revile you and persecute you" (Matthew 5:11, 12). He didn't say, "Go tell them that they are forgiven."

When Jesus forgave, his forgiveness was something between himself and God: "Father, forgive them for they know not what they do." The appropriate response is to forgive prayerfully, to let the attitude of forgiveness become an interior affair of the heart. When this has happened, forgiveness will become an external expression of the hand. One's forgiveness is expressed to others, not in verbal affirmations, but in concrete actions of love.

"I forgive you" is not something we say to others. "Father, forgive them" is what we more properly should say to God. When we can say that, when that is the true attitude of our hearts, then forgiveness will be expressed in our actions toward those who have offended us. Saying "I forgive you" is too easy; living "I forgive you" is much more difficult.

How to fall without breaking something important? Forgive. Get a forgiving attitude! Express a forgiving attitude.

Stuck in Neutral: Forgiving Myself

Sometimes forgiveness must start with me. I must give myself the freedom to fall, the latitude to make mistakes. If I can't forgive myself, my spiritual life, not to speak of my relational life, is stuck in neutral. It ain't going nowhere. And, unfortunately, I tend to bring others into my spiritual malaise.

Brooding over my falls and failures is like spinning my wheels; I'm expending a lot of energy but going nowhere. I'm making a lot of noise, but digging a deeper rut. And those who are back there trying to get me out of the mess are only getting a lot of mud in their faces.

- Forgiveness is getting back to square one so I can get on to square two.
- Forgiving myself allows me to kick the gear shift into drive.
- Forgiving myself allows me to begin work on other projects in my life.

God Is in the Forgiveness Business

Forgiveness is an attitude of faith whereby I turn over to God the business of how the other guy is doing. Yes, he did me a bad turn. Yes, she "tore out my heart and stomped that sucker flat." Yes, he is not a very nice person. Forgiveness is letting God deal with it. God is in the business; I'm not.

Forgiveness Is not Forgetting

Although Henry Ward Beecher said in his *Life Thoughts* that being able to forgive but not forget is just another way of saying "I cannot forgive," Beecher is wrong. *Forgiveness is not saying "forget it."* Forgiveness is not saying "I forget." Forgiveness is not saying "It's okay." Rather, forgiveness is saying "I'm okay, and I am willing to let God deal with whether you are okay, and I am also willing to let go of my need to be the instrument of correction and rebuke in your life."

Ouch! That's hard. We want to be right there when God settles the score. We want to be on hand to see the other guy get his. God says, "Nope! Go to your room, while I deal with your brother." Forgiveness is not only going off to our room while God handles the situation, but going willingly and gratefully, thankful we have a God we can trust implicitly.

Forgiveness Is not Numbness

Forgiveness is not saying "I no longer feel the pain." Rather, forgiveness is saying "I no longer feel the need to hold on to your involvement in my pain."

Incredibly, we often want to hold on to our bitterness and resentment. Like an arrow shot into our side, if we hold on to it, we can keep it from moving and causing more pain. Forgiveness is the willingness to pull it out, let it go. Yes, there may be a scar for life; yes, we may never be the same. Yet, forgiving the person for the pain is another way of saying "I am no longer involved with you in my pain. I can deal with my pain without having any further issues with you."

This is Jesus on the cross. "Father, forgive them," he said, as they laughed at his naked humiliation. "Father, forgive them," he said, even as the nails twisted in his hands. He was able to separate the instruments of his pain from the pain itself. He could forgive. This is the good news. William Blake puts it this way:

> What can this gospel of Jesus be?
> What life and immortality?
> What was it that he brought to light
> That Plato and Cicero did not write?
>
> Then Jesus rose and said to me,
> "Thy sins are all forgiven thee."[1]

God Leads a Pretty Sheltered Life

Does God have a right to expect us to forgive unconditionally? A modern parable addresses this question. At the end of time, billions of people were scattered on a great plain before God's throne. Some of the groups near the front talked heatedly—not with cringing shame, but with belligerence.

"How can God judge us? How can he know about suffering?" snapped a weary survivor of Buchenwald. She jerked back a sleeve to reveal a tattooed number from a Nazi concentration camp. "We endured terror, beating, torture, and death!"

In another group, a black man lowered his collar. "What about this?" he demanded, showing an ugly rope burn. "Lynched for no crime but being black! We have suffocated in slave ships, been wrenched from loved ones, toiled till only death gave release."

Far out across the plain were hundreds of such groups. Each had a complaint against God for the evil and suffering God permitted in this world. How lucky God was to live in heaven, where all was sweetness and light, where there was no weeping, no fear, no hunger, no hatred. Indeed, what did God know about what humans had been forced to endure in this world? "After all, God leads a pretty sheltered life," they said.

So each group sent out a leader, chosen because he or she had suffered the most. There was a Jew, a black, an untouchable from India, an illegitimate, a homosexual, a survivor of Hiroshima, a prisoner from a Siberian slave camp. In the center of the plain they consulted with each other. At last they were ready to present their case. It was rather simple: Before God would be qualified to be their judge, God must endure what they had endured. Their decision was that God "should be sentenced to live on earth—as a human!"

But, because this was God, they set certain safeguards to be sure God could not use divine powers on God's own behalf.

Let him be born a Jew.

Let the legitimacy of his birth be doubted. Let him champion a cause so just, but so radical that it brings down upon him the hate, condemnation, and opposition of every major traditional political, social, and religious authority.

Let him try to describe what no person has ever seen, tasted, heard, or smelled—let him try to communicate God to humankind.

Let him be indicted on false charges.

Let him be tried before a prejudiced jury and convicted by a cowardly judge.

Let him see what it is to be terribly alone and completely abandoned by everyone.

Let him be tortured.

Let him die a humiliating death, and let it be with common criminals.

As each leader announced his portion of the sentence, loud murmurs of approval went up from the great throng of people. When the last had finished pronouncing the sentence, there was a long silence. No one uttered another word. No one moved. For suddenly all knew: God had already served the sentence.

The Future of Forgiveness

Because of that pivotal moment in history when Jesus completed his "sentence," we are able to make choices.

The face of revenge looks toward the past; it is fixated on something that happened "back then" or "back there."

The face of forgiveness looks toward the future. It is transfixed on the possibilities that lie on the horizon; it sees the potential that can never be realized when one is wearing the mask of revenge and looking backward.

No one illustrated this better than Joseph Cardinal Bernadin, the late Archbishop of Chicago. After serious allegations of sexual misconduct were publicly aired, he steadfastly asserted his innocence without vilifying the accuser. When the accuser later recanted his testimony, the cardinal extended his gracious forgiveness and acknowledged that the young man had been in his prayers daily.

The first lesson in learning to fall is how to forgive. The falls in our life cannot be redeemed without forgiveness happening somewhere, at some point.

NOTE

[1]William Blake, "The Everlasting Gospel," in *The Selected Poetry and Prose of Blake,* Northrop Frye, ed. (New York: The Modern Library, 1953), pp. 317–318.

14

Apologize

The students in my conflict resolution class looked at me incredulously, as though I had just suggested that the moon was made of cream cheese after all. "Apologize?" one asked. "How can you apologize for something you didn't do?"

I had mentioned the dreaded A word. After spending hours discussing various negotiation strategies, win-lose situations, fighting fair, assertive versus aggressive behaviors, I mention this one little word as a possible solution to many conflicts, and the class is totally disbelieving. It was at this moment that I first began to wonder if we have forgotten or lost the art of apologizing.

"If you didn't do anything, don't apologize," I said to this student. "But if you are in conflict with someone, isn't it possible that you also share some of the responsibility for the conflict? Apologize for your role in creating the conflict, or contributing to the escalation of it."

The word "apology" comes from the Latin *apologia*, meaning "defense." When John Cardinal Newman wrote his *Apologia Pro Sua Vita* (Apology for My Life), he was writing a memoir, an explanation, and was not in the modern parlance apologizing for anything. However, when the U.S. government apologizes to the Native American Indian nations, or when the United Church of Christ offered an apology to indigenous Hawaiian people several years ago, it was not a defense or an explanation, but rather a sincere statement of regret.

Apologies, however, are rare in public and private discourse. Perhaps we think we are quite willing to apologize for our behavior, but often what we want to pass off as an apology is not an apology at all, but a passive-aggressive way of reasserting our innocence.

The Non-Apology

The most common form of the non-apology is the expression "I'm sorry." No two words roll off the tongue so easily when push comes to shove than the words I'm sorry, and no two words have been so emptied of their meaning. To say "I'm sorry" has become a sort of mantra that is reflexively uttered whenever the situation careens in a direction we had not anticipated. We knock over a glass of milk. I'm sorry. We speak crossly to our mates. I'm sorry. We selfishly insist on our own way. I'm sorry. We do not call when we're going to be late. I'm sorry.

Soon, not only has "I'm sorry" become a meaningless expression, but it has been further reduced to simply "Sorry." Now we don't even remind ourselves and our victim that it is I who is sorry. It's not "*I'm* sorry." Now it's simply "Sorry."

"Sorry" is self-righteousness dressed up as an apology. It is not an apology; at best it is a relational Band-Aid that does nothing to address the cause of the wound.

The Doormat Apology

This apology is uttered by the person who insists on keeping the peace no matter what. The issue of who is really at fault and who is the offender is irrelevant. The apology gets uttered by the "doormat" for no other reason than that an apology must be offered by someone—anyone.

If you're a Boomer or older, you remember Norman Lear's groundbreaking television sitcom "All in the Family." Jean Stapleton and Carroll O'Connor played Archie and Edith Bunker, a husband and wife duo known for Archie's outbursts and Edith's compliant behavior. In one scene, Amelia, a friend of Edith's, comments on Archie and Edith's marriage: "Of all the people I know, you're practically the only one who has a happy marriage."

"Really? Me and Archie? Oh, thank you."

"What's your secret Edith?"

"Oh, I ain't got no secret. Archie and me still have our fights. Of course, we don't let them go on too long. Somebody always says "I'm sorry," and then Archie always says, "It's okay, Edith.""

A Child's Apology

Children, when apprehended in a crime of passion, like taking a fistful of cookies from the cookie sheet just minutes out of the oven, will need little prompting to say "I'm sorry." What is often meant, however, is "How could I have been so stupid as to get caught?" When Jay Leno asked Hugh Grant, "What were you thinking?" Grant's response was the equivalent of, "I have no idea." He was clearly embarrassed, not with his lack of moral character, but that he had been apprehended.

Excuse me!

Sometimes, we go beyond the non-apology to something more creative. It goes something like this: "I'm sorry you took offense when I said you needed to control your children better, because when they're out of control as teenagers, they're gone, and that's right where your kids are heading. If you can't take a little constructive advice, and if you are so sensitive that what I said offended you, and if you are so insecure that you can't handle a little help from your friends, then excuuuuse me! I apologize!" What kind of apology is that? It's no apology. It's a frontal assault on a person's dignity and self-esteem. It's a thinly disguised justification for boorishness.

Pat Boone used the Excuse Me apology in 1997 after he appeared in a heavy-metal act dressed in leather, dark glasses, and earrings at the January 1997 American Music Awards. Trinity Broadcasting Network peevishly cancelled his "Gospel America" program. A few days later, Boone issued a statement: "To whatever extent somebody was wounded...I am sorry. I don't apologize for the music, I don't apologize for making the appearance on the show. But for whatever negative fallout there might have been, I regret that. I've eaten some crow, and it's delicious."

The Nixonian Apology

The "I am not a crook" apology is a form of denial. It goes like this: "I'm sorry for the pain I have caused, which if I had truly caused, I would be truly sorry for, and I can understand how upset you are, just as I am, but I am sorry for this pain that you feel I have inflicted upon you even if I haven't."

The Wine-and-Roses Apology

You've had words, and he returns later with a bottle of wine and some roses. Perhaps he even cooks dinner, sets the table, and invites you to sit down and eat the repast he has prepared. A dozen red roses adorn the table, and you think you're eating with the Red Baron. Who is this stranger at your table?

And that is precisely the problem. The Wine and Roses approach, while extremely pleasant, leaves issues unresolved. On the upside, if the same issue stays unresolved, it may portend an unlimited number of romantic candlelight evenings, and perhaps it is not an issue that should be resolved!

The Offhand Apology

This non-apology pretends that you're totally unaware of how this happened. The child drops a plate of food on the floor. "How did that happen?" he says. "Oops!"

The "oops" apology says, "Oops! Sorry about that." Bought that new Miata convertible without talking it over with you? Did I do that? Oops! I'm sorry. Tossed out that ratty old sweater of yours that you've been keeping in the closet since you graduated from SMU? Oops! I'm sorry. Didn't tell you I was bringing colleagues home for dinner to-night? Oops! I'm sorry! Didn't let you know we were having a staff meeting at 1 p.m. today? Oops! I'm sorry.

The Self-Serving Apology

This apology sees an opportunity to do "damage control" by spin-ning the experience into something positive. The words "apologize" or "regret" may be used, but the larger goal is to use the apology as a means of self-aggrandizement.

"I'm sorry, but the reason this happened was that I was only trying to help. And if you would only realize what a great person I am and stop insisting on being so petty about this, this whole thing would blow over and we could get on with it."

In March 1996, Mahmoud Abdul-Rauf was a point guard for the Denver Nuggets. A devout Muslim, he had for some time taken the position that he could no longer stand for the national anthem of a country whose oppressive policies he was in fundamental disagreement with. No one had really noticed until the NBA issued an ultimatum requiring him to stand. He agreed to stand, but said what while standing he would be praying.

The story hit the local and national papers and a controversy ensued. One Friday morning deejays from a local Denver radio station walked into the mosque on Parker Road in Denver, cranked up their radios, and created general mayhem as part of an early-morning radio stunt. Their actions disturbed people who were praying (Friday is a holy day for Muslims), and Muslims, along with the Denver community, were outraged. A week later, the parent company of the radio station took out a full page ad in the *Rocky Mountain News*. As a part of the "apology" they noted that the stunt was unauthorized, it was "not encouraged or condoned" by the management, and "overshadowed the many good works KBPI, its employees, and the other Jacor radio stations undertake in this community." It went on to identify "active involvement in many community groups," public affairs programming, sponsorship of and contribution to numerous events and fundraisers, civic involvement, the "Grand Halo Award" for contributions to the Safe Summer program, and the station's work with the Community Partnership Office. Many readers of this apology spin were left with the queasy feeling that the station just didn't "get it."

These non-apologies achieve what they are intended to do: minimize the damage, defect criticism, allow life to go on without being delayed by relational anxieties and busywork. They are the functional equivalent of cleaning the windshield when what the car needs is more gas.

Learning to fall means learning to apologize. The only thing one needs to learn how to do to apologize is to ask the question: What do I want this apology to achieve? What we want is for things to be the way they were before, or better. Perhaps the way things were is not a good goal. But an effective apology gets us back to the point where we were, even if that point was not a good place to be, and then allows us to move to a better place.

There are three things that must be present in an apology for it to help you get up and still look good: confession, closure, and change.

Confession

A good apology always acknowledges responsibility. Make it personal. "Mistakes were made" is not enough. Try, "I was wrong. I did it. I screwed up. That's my handiwork! The buck stops here." Your confession does not need to be expressed in Elizabethan prose. A simple "I made a mistake" or "I'm the one responsible" will work nicely. Just think of how uttering simple confessional words like this can make a difference. What if Nixon had simply said on the day after the break-in: "This is a major disaster, and I'm the one responsible." He would have finished his term.

You'll never look better in the eyes of your peers at the office or your family at home than when you've taken a tumble, you're lying there in a heap of trouble with ski poles and skis all over the place, and you simply acknowledge what everyone else in the whole world, especially your family, already knows: "I screwed up!"

Refusing to take responsibility makes it much more difficult for the situation to be redeemed. You're lying in the snow and someone skis over to help you. You say, "It's okay. I didn't fall. Just hit a little bump there. No problem. I can get up. Where's my right leg? Did I run into you?" The reality is that on a ski slope there is very little another skier can do to help a fellow skier up, except to provide advice and moral support. In the absence of an admission of a problem, there's no reason for anyone to get involved. It would only create a bigger pile-up in an already congested area. People are quite willing to help you when you want to be helped and when you are willing to acknowledge your role. Your confession is an indication to others that you are willing to work on this. That is a signal for them to step to your side and give you some help.

Jim Bakker of PTL fame had as spectacular a fall as public figures can have. The title of his book? *I Was Wrong.* The book has generally received high marks for its forthrightness, and the public perception of Bakker has slowly been changing. Contrast this to the series of books by those involved in the ill-fated prosecution of O. J. Simpson. None of the principals take responsibility without attempting to shift responsibility to other parties. Chris Darden and Marcia Clark would have been better served to write an apology for their own behavior, rather than that of others. A book like that would sell.

Closure

The situation can be brought to resolution by asking for a response. This is the really tough part of an apology. To provide closure, you must ask for forgiveness.

Yes, ask for forgiveness. You admit responsibility, and then you say, "Will you forgive me?" Four very difficult words to say. One reason they are so hard to say is that they express neediness. You need to be forgiven. You are at your absolute weakest now. You are vulnerable. You have already said that you are the stupid person who did the stupid thing. Now you open yourself up even further to ask for the injured party's forgiveness.

This person or persons have the option of saying no. They may refuse you. They may say, "You know, Timothy, right now I am so angry I am in no mood to even think about forgiveness." Or they may say, "Forget it. You think you can do this and then get off by saying you're sorry and asking me to forgive you? Forget it."

Those are the kinds of responses you may get. Falling and getting up gracefully, however, involves this step: asking for forgiveness. What you accomplish by asking for forgiveness is that the responsibility for healing the relationship is now taken from you and given to others. There is nothing further you can do (assuming you have made reparations for actual physical or financial damages that may have occurred). Perhaps you will never be forgiven by this party. This is okay. Their unwillingness to forgive you is not your problem, and you should now let it go. It is their problem. The choice to live with bitterness and resentment is theirs to make. You have done what you should do when you fall in life, as everyone does: You have taken responsibility and you have requested forgiveness.

Most of the time, however, the response you get will be, "Of course I forgive you." When you get that sort of response, the relationship, whether at the office or at home, heals, and you are able to move on. You have achieved closure on this incident. You are standing up, perhaps wobbly, but looking good, ready to continue down the slopes!

When I apologize to my wife or my children I always ask them to forgive me. I do it because I want this to be over. I want to know where I stand. I want closure. I want to move on.

I also do it because I know it helps the family member deal with the situation I have created. Now, they must think about it and they must deal with it. When Jeanie says yes, I know she's ready and willing to move on. And when she says yes, she knows she is making a commitment to move on.

Moreover, asking forgiveness of the children is a way to model how to deal with the falls of life. I believe my kids are learning from my example. The fact that I make mistakes is not upsetting to them. Kids have an intuitive understanding about human nature. When I show them that the way you handle your mistakes is to 'fess up and get a response, they learn something important: that it's no humiliation to fall, and it's not so hard to get up. The most important thing in life is learning how to fall, and how to get up.

In the work place, however, I do not always say, "Will you forgive me?" In my professional life, to say that sounds a bit cloying, and it has a theological flavor that does not always seem appropriate. It's just too unreal. I don't want to be freaking people out. So, instead, I use different words to say the same thing. I say, "I'm really sorry about the mix-up. Totally my fault. Can you cut me some slack on this one?" Or, if the situation caused by my incompetence is really bad, I say, "Do you think we could start over?"

People usually respond to someone who's lying in a pile of snow obviously messed up and who is now extending a hand for some help. Asking for a response is the equivalent to extending a hand for help. Someone will usually extend theirs and get you back on your feet again. Closure.

Change

A good apology seeks change. The negative experience can be shape-shifted to become a positive one. An apology with a confession and request for forgiveness can reshape the experience and turn a possible failure into a redemptive fall.

Angeles Arrien, in her essay "Walking the Mystical Path with Practical Feet," describes an experience that she was able to reshape. She was

at a bus stop sitting next to a woman reading a newspaper. While waiting for the bus, she became engrossed in the performance of a fourteen-
year-old boy on a skateboard. He had his baseball cap on backward, and
he was skating beautifully and very fast. A couple of times he came by
where the women were sitting and buzzed them, very nearly hitting
them. On a third pass, he accidentally knocked the newspaper out of
the woman's hands. She said, "Oh, why don't you grow up?" Arrien
writes:

> I watched him glide down to the corner of the block, where he
> stood talking with his buddy. The two of them kept looking
> back over their shoulders at the woman. She hesitated for a
> moment, then rolled up her paper, tucked it under her arm and
> walked into the street motioning to him. "Why don't you come
> here?" she called. "I want to talk to you."
>
> Very reluctantly, he skated over to her, turned his cap around
> with the bill in front, and said, "Yeah?"
>
> She said, "What I meant to say was that I was afraid that I
> might get hurt. I apologize for what I did say."
>
> His face lit up and he said, "How cool!"
>
> In that moment, I witnessed what is called in Spanish a *milagro
> pequeno*—a small miracle. This small miracle was a holy healing
> moment between generations, between two human beings who
> had just become important strangers to each other. The woman
> chose to shift the shape of her experience by moving out of
> reactivity to creativity.[1]

Learning to fall requires forgiveness; it also requires apology. We
must learn how to shape-shift our falls, so that they are truly falls, not
failures, from which we can arise to continue on our life's journey.

NOTE

[1]Angeles Arrien, "Walking the Mystical Path with Practical Feet," in *Nourishing the Soul*,
Anne Simpkinson et al., eds. (San Francisco: HarperSanFrancisco, 1995), p. 104.

15

Learn

Some of us learn to grow beyond the way we were taught.
—Barbara Blaisdell's mother[1]

Four monkeys were put into a room. In the center of the room was a tall pole with a bunch of bananas suspended from the top. One particularly hungry monkey eagerly scrambled up the pole, intent on retrieving a banana. Just as he reached out to grasp the banana, he was hit with a torrent of cold water from an overhead shower nozzle. With a squeal, the monkey abandoned its quest and retreated down the pole. Each monkey attempted in turn to secure a banana. Each received an equally chilly shower, and each scampered down without the prize. After repeated drenchings, the monkeys finally gave up on the bananas.

With the primates thus conditioned, one of the original four was removed from the experiment and a new monkey added. No sooner had this new, innocent monkey started up the pole than his (or her) companions reached up and yanked the surprised creature back down the pole. The monkey got the message—Don't climb the pole. After a few such aborted attempts, but without ever getting a cold shower, the new monkey stopped trying to get the bananas. One by one, each of the original monkeys was replaced. Each new monkey learned the same lesson: Don't climb the pole. None of the new monkeys ever made it to the top of the pole; none even got so far as a cold shower. Not one understood precisely why pole climbing was discouraged, but they all respected the well-established precedent. Even after the shower was removed, no monkey ventured up the pole.

Banana Thinking

My friend Kevin confided once that the most shattering experience of his life came when he realized that there were other ways of doing things! "I learned I had to change, and I had to unlearn that I had all the answers," he said ruefully after a painful experience.

What Kevin had to unlearn was *banana thinking*, that is, the uncritical acceptance of the ideas by which we order our lives. The four most influential monkeys in our life that pull us off the pole of creative and post-conventional thinking are:

The Guilt Monkey—Unlearn Guilt; Learn Grace

Sometimes we are not conscious of the way the past affects our present behavior and attitudes. A young mother loved to bake chicken, and when she prepared it for the oven she always cut off the hind quarter and then put it in the pan. Once, when her mother saw her doing this, she asked, "Why on earth are you cutting off the hind quarter like that?" The daughter, taken aback, said, "Because that's the way I always saw you cooking chicken." The mother laughed and said, "I did that because I never had a pan big enough to cook a whole chicken."

Do you still believe it is better for leftovers to cool off on the counter before putting them in the refrigerator? That practice

---

BANANA THINKING: 10 CORE PRINCIPLES

There are many principles of banana thinking. Here are a few of the important ones:

- We've never done it that way before.
- Nobody has done it that way before.
- It has been done before.
- It didn't work then; it won't work now.
- It should be referred to committee.
- I need to get some sleep on it first.
- The boss will never go for it.
- You're right, but...
- It's too radical.
- I'm too old for this.
- The janitor says it can't be done.
- If it's not broke...
- If you'd suggested that last month, I'd say...
- It's not our problem.
- We have a policy against that.

dates back several generations to when great-grandma had an icebox. Putting warm or hot foods in the icebox was not a good idea because the block of ice would melt!

Because the past is the repository of all the lessons we have learned and the experiences we have suffered through, it may begin to assume the character of the sacred. The past represents our accumulated wisdom stored in an ever-growing temple of tradition. It is not to be tampered with, and attempts to depart from its wisdom are often treated as profane and foolish.

If the past doesn't contain our wisdom, it may preserve our failures. The bitter memory of these lapses and the guilt that goes along with it prevent us from abandoning banana thinking; we cannot break from our past, and consequently our past breaks us.

We can beat the Guilt Monkey in a couple of ways: The apostle Paul suggests that we "forget" the past. But to do this, two other things must happen. First, we must have a goal toward which we are striving. In Paul's case, this was the "mark of the high calling of God in Christ Jesus." Second, we must understand what he means by "forget." He doesn't really mean "forget." He means "disregard." If we have a goal before us, it is now time to disregard what has gone on in the past. It is useless information. You can't turn back the clock, but you can wind it up again. The past may inform, teach, and generate renewed resolution and determination, but it need not keep us from achieving our goals. That's why Rabbi Mordecai Kaplan said that the "past has a vote, but not a veto."

Kevin, to whom I referred above, and his wife Rachel both have been married before; she twice, he once. Marriage, understandably, was a thoughtful step for them this time. But after many years of marriage together, they both are now able to look dispassionately on where they've been and how they got there. Rachel makes the point that she and Kevin have more "disagreements" than she ever had in either of her previous marriages. But she attributes this not to a weakness in the marriage, but to the strength of the trust they have in each other and in the relationship. "I have finally been able to let go of the past," she says, "because I now have an opportunity to transcend it. I can say 'I've been there, done that' and it really has no bearing on my life with Kevin now."

I strongly believe that Paul's suggestion is great advice for a postmodern world afflicted by dysfunctional families, codependency disorders, drug therapies, and millennial fever. The past, rather than acting as a prison where the self is bound and tormented, must more closely resemble a library where one can go for self-revelation and information. The present and the future far outrank the past; that is why the apostle says that one must examine the past, and then regard it ultimately as so much garbage that has no relevancy for the push toward the goal.

Richard Bach, author of many books, including *Jonathan Livingston Seagull*, has another suggestion in his book *Illusions*. He advises us to create or "choose" our past.[2] The experiences of today become the past of tomorrow. That being so, it is possible to create or choose the past we will have tomorrow. If we make wrong choices today, tomorrow we will wake up to a past of wrong choices and bad experiences. But if we make good choices today, if we choose to live this day with joy, if we should be true to our values, then tomorrow we will wake up to a beautiful past that is not condemning but affirming, not limiting but freeing, not of guilt but of grace.

The Hostile Monkey—Unlearn Aggressiveness; Learn Assertiveness

The aggressive person is still at the base of the pole yanking others off; the assertive person affirms his or her right to climb. The aggressive person needs to be in control and uses coercive behaviors to get the desired result. The assertive person is not interested in control, only in outcomes. This can be achieved without abusive language or behavior. If you'd like your spouse to clean out the garage, you make a simple declarative statement to that effect. That's assertive behavior. Raising your voice is aggressive behavior. If you want your child to clean his or her room, you make a simple declarative statement. That's assertive behavior. Calling the child a filthy slob is abusive behavior.

Use the X-PROFILE® to act assertively:

Step One: X-AMINE the Circumstances. Provide a description of the problem or situation. Avoid using inflammatory words or pushing someone's "hot" buttons. This is merely an explanatory step. You explain how you see the situation.

Step Two: X-PRESS your Concern. State how this makes you feel. Does the person's behavior make you feel angry, hurt, wounded, that you are unimportant, that she or he doesn't consider your needs or concerns? Say so.

Step Three: X-PECT Change. State what you want to happen. Be specific. It may be wise to offer a range of choices. But if this is impossible, make it clear precisely what it is you want to change and see happen.

Wrong: I want you to be more considerate.

Right: I want you to call when you're going to be late.

Wrong: I want you to help more around the house.

Right: Here's the vacuum.

Wrong: I want you to lighten up.

Right: I want you to tell me you love me when you're having a bad day.

Step Four: X-PLAIN the Consequences. If there are no consequences for the failure to provide the change you are seeking, you may not get the change you want. Explain what you intend to do if the unwanted behavior or activity does not stop. Be creative! Make certain, however, that the consequences you describe are reasonable and enforceable.

Weak

"You're grounded for two months!" (Improbable)

"I'll never speak to you again." (Impulsive and childish)

"I'm going to take this all the way to the Supreme Court!" (A consequence over which you have no control)

"You'll never do business in this town again." (Vindictive)

"Santa won't bring you any presents." (Mean)

"You'll go to bed without supper." (Abusive)

Strong

"I'll hide the remote control." (Ouch!)

"You'll have to go shopping with me." (Oh, no! Not that!)

"I'll file a grievance with the ____ agency." (Okay, okay)

"No video games tomorrow." (Ah, come on!)

"I will not accept work if it is late." (Even if the dog ate my homework?)

"You will not be able to go to the game." (You wouldn't!)

"I'll play Frank Sinatra music." (Who?)

"You'll have to spend your own allowance to replace it." (Not fair!)

Step Five: X-ECUTE Control! Prepare to follow through on the consequences outlined in Step Four. Without follow-through, an assertive strategy becomes an accommodation device that undermines future attempts to gain control of your life.

Step Six: X-UDE Confidence! Carry yourself with poise. The X-PROFILE® enables you to establish control in areas of your life that need to be brought into control. It does so without offending the dignity or personhood of others, while at the same time allowing you to set boundaries and limits with firmness and strength. You have every reason to be confident because you know that if you meet resistance, you are prepared to put into place the consequences you have described; and if you do not meet resistance, you will have achieved something a compliant person or aggressive person might not have achieved.

The Christian has a further obligation, however. Assertive strategies must be conducted in love. Assertiveness must target the behavior, not the person. Aggressive attitudes focus on the person; assertive strategies focus on the behavior.

The Conventional Monkey— Unlearn Left-Brain; Learn Right-Brain

In the '80s, *Cheers!* along with *The Cosby Show,* was one of the hit situation comedies on television. Part of the fun of watching *Cheers!* was to observe the interaction between Sam Malone, played by Ted Danson, and Diane Chambers, played by Shelly Long. Sam, always going with his right-brain instincts, if not some other, less noble instinct, was continually frustrated by Diane's overweening need to analyze things before surrendering to her emotions. At the very moment when Sam believed

---

BANANA THINKING AT HOME

She says:

- We can't afford it.
- What about the kids?
- Couldn't we discuss this first?
- I've changed my mind.
- It's not practical.
- Let's wait until it's on sale.
- Couldn't we get this in another color?

He says:

- It doesn't have a remote control.
- We don't need another bathroom; what we need is an RV.
- Let me think about it and I'll let you know.
- I know where I'm going, thank you very much.
- No thanks, I don't need any help.
- I told you once I love you; if I change my mind, I'll let you know.
- I like it just the way it is.

that Diane was about to succumb to a romantic impulse, her left-brain took over and the mood was destroyed.

On the other hand, we may need to unlearn right-brain and learn left-brain. If the left-brain person tends to make decisions with passionless reason, the right-brain person is making decisions with reasonless passion. We are often either coldly calculating without the softening effect of passion, or we are maudlin muddlers suffering from brain drain.

The Grudge Monkey—Unlearn Resentment; Learn Forgiveness

Once, when in conversation with some friends about resentment and forgiveness, Ruthanne made it very clear: "I'm a grudge-holder," she announced. Her husband, sitting nearby, nodded in agreement. "I can still remember who grabbed my place in the lunch line in first grade!" Ruthanne clearly was no longer afflicted by this particular resentment, but she is able to understand that it is her nature to hold resentments for a long period of time. Learning forgiveness is difficult for her, but fortunately, she has a husband who gently helps her overcome her resentments, even the ones that he himself may have caused!

The Materialistic Monkey—Unlearn Success; Learn Courage

More "successful" business people than ever are leaving the rat race for the human race, opting out of conventional perceptions of success and embracing instead a simple lifestyle that stresses quality rather than quantity.

Faith Popcorn, in her book *The Popcorn Report*, describes ten trends that are affecting life in the last decade of the millennium. Of these ten, two are related to quality-of-life issues. The "Small Indulgences" trend is seen in the desire to satisfy the inner motivation of "I deserve it." Crucial to this trend is quality: value and intrinsic worth versus image and name. A second trend focusing on quality of life is what she calls "Cashing Out," an emphasis on living now—long and well. Those who "cash out" are willing to swap the traditional success prizes for a slower pace.[3]

Boston Chicken experienced phenomenal growth in its early history. Then after laying a few rotten eggs, it fell on hard times. They had bloated costs, poor marketing decisions, and in consequence, a plummeting stock price. At the moment when Boston Chicken was bottoming out, the CEO, Scott Beck, spoke to a group of Boston Chicken muckety-mucks, and confessed, "Clearly, this has been a low point in my business career. But with all of this, you have to get up and move forward because people are counting on you. These are people who believe in you and believe in your dreams. With dreams come costs."[4]

He then went on to quote Winston Churchill: "Success is never final. Failure is never fatal. What's important is courage."[5]

It takes courage to see "success" and "failure" for what they are. It takes courage to insist on being true to yourself, whatever the cost.

In his book *Markings*, his diary from the days when he was Secretary General of the United Nations, Dag Hammarskjold remarked:

> Don't be afraid to be yourself, live your individuality to the full— but for the good of others. Don't copy others in order to buy fellowship, or make convention your law instead of living the righteousness.
>
> To become free and responsible. For this alone was man created, and he who fails to take the Way which could have been his shall be lost eternally.[6]

The Sexist Monkey—Unlearn Gender Roles; Learn Bender Roles

Women have a uterus; they can give birth to a child. Apart from that rather significant difference between the sexes, there is little else in relational life that is gender specific. Of course, there are well-documented gender proclivities and styles in communication, nurturing, and physical activities. But if you say to your spouse one evening after work, "Can I help you get dinner?" you are implicitly implying that "getting dinner" is the other person's role, for which you have now magnanimously offered assistance. Feeding the baby, changing the oil, vacuuming, ironing, laundry, washing the car, mowing the lawn, making coffee, and making beds are not gender-specific tasks. Get over it.

Having said that—studies show that households work best where the roles are understood. The point here, however, is that the roles need not be apportioned along gender lines. It is important to remember also that the allocation of these duties will need to be adjusted from time to time depending on a variety of possible circumstances: a new job, a baby, illness, and so on.

The Talking Monkey—Unlearn Arrogance;
Learn Listening

We do not learn well in a vacuum. Feedback is critically important in learning how to fall. Feedback feeds back to us perceptions and observations that we ourselves cannot possibly gain when we are going through a difficult time.

We are not required to value all feedback equally. Nor are we required to act upon all feedback. We are required to listen to feedback without slashing back defensively when it is given. Feedback, rather than being imposed upon us, should be actively sought by us. This is particularly true if we have friends who can provide feedback honestly.

I didn't say that friends will give us *honest* feedback, but give us feedback *honestly*. No person can provide a viewpoint that is completely objective. Every person's feedback is skewed in one direction or another. That's why you may decide that a friend's perspective, while valuable, is not useful in your case. But friends can provide feedback in an honest manner that has integrity and value.

A factor that makes the delivery of feedback difficult is our diminishing conversational skills. In a time when electronic technology makes communication easier, we have made conversation harder. Expressing our thoughts in a bi-directional conversation is an experience that we do not do well. What makes a good conversation?

When we have a conversation with another person or persons we bring to the table all that we are as individuals ourselves. The complex persons we are is a mix of cultural, educational, environmental, religious, ethnic, and gender strands. We respond in conversation in unique conversational fingerprints that others in the conversation learn to recognize and sometimes exploit.

But we also rely on our values and traditions and experiences to inform us as we critically reflect on the issues that we lay on the table.

Some of us come to the conversation table with our minds made up. When we fall, it is important to learn how to discuss the experience and the decisions that might emerge from it. Conversations with others help us to reflect on what happened and what we can learn.

- When we have this conversation we must be interested in dialogue and not monologue. That is, we must be willing to spend as much time, perhaps more, listening than we do speaking.

- We must also not give in to the temptation to argue, but rather to explore. Therefore, a good conversation can only take place when some level of disinterest has been reached. Sometimes a cooling off period is necessary before such a dialogue can take place.
- We must be willing to test hypotheses.
- We need to ask questions.
- We need to respect other opinions.
- We must focus on words, not on personalities.
- We need to understand that a conversation is not a judicial proceeding, but a scientific inquiry into the nature of truth.
- We must choose words carefully.
- We must avoid superlatives and generalizations. "Every time I want to go out, you say that…"
- We must acknowledge the other person's feelings.
- We must be willing to accept a different point of view.
- We must remember that the goal is to "get up and look good." No one looks better than when he or she admits an error and appears determined to correct it. In other words, humility wears much better than pride. Nietzsche had it right when he said, "It seems to me so foolish to wish to be right at the cost of love."
- We must be willing to defend our opinion but only in the interest of *exploring* truth, not *imposing* truth.
- We must be willing to challenge a statement, not in the interest of being right, but in searching for new meaning.
- We must be willing to acknowledge ambiguity. The "either-or" fallacy easily creeps into disagreeable conversations. Sometimes reality is ambiguous; admitting the ambiguity and agreeing to live with it is occasionally the answer.
- We must be willing to enlarge the conversational matrix. Sometimes two people cannot seem to see beyond the forest. Bringing more people into the conversation can clarify issues.
- We should converse in the interest of clarification, not justification.

- We must recognize that in conversation we are permitted only to expose others to our point of view, not impose that view. To do the first is to have convictions, to attempt the latter is to be dogmatic.

It is helpful to remember the Socratic confession: "I know that I do not know." Nicholas of Cusa expressed the same thought in the phrase "learned ignorance."

The Newspaper Wars

For a long time, Jeanie and I fought over the newspaper. Yes, the newspaper. I am a "clipper." I see an article that interests me, and I tear it out of the paper immediately for filing. Jeanie then comes across the mutilated paper and is frustrated because her right to read a virgin newspaper has been precluded by my avaricious need to clip and snip. For a long time we ordered both of the local dailies, the *Rocky Mountain News* and the *Denver Post*. She read the one, I the other. We stopped our subscription to one of the papers, however, because the service was so bad. That left us with only one paper. A dangerous situation!

One day we were both reading the Sunday paper at the kitchen table. I saw something of interest, and knowing if I didn't clip it then I'd forget what I'd seen and lose it, I ruthlessly tore it out and set it aside. "Why don't you just tear the whole page?" Jeanie asked.

I was ready for her. "If I don't tear it out now, I forget where it was," I explained, irritated. She grimaced and went on reading, her obvious discomfort enflamed by smoldering resentment about the entire arrangement. I pushed away from the table and said, "I don't know why this is such a big deal. When you're clipping coupons, I don't raise a fuss." I moved toward the door, and as I was leaving, I turned and delivered a parting shot: "We'll just order two identical papers, and that will solve the problem!"

Of course, the problem was not solved. I could tell that Jeanie was still internalizing the sharp words we had exchanged. Later that day in the garden, I asked her how it was going.

"Fine—"

"But," I interrupted. "But what?"

"This newspaper thing…" Ha! She was going to apologize for her inconsiderate position! She went on, "I just don't understand why you can't tear the page out and set it aside."

She sandbagged me! She had made that very suggestion earlier, hadn't she? Tear the entire page! That way I have my article, and, at the same time, she can read the page on both sides too. I looked at her, stunned, and then said, "Well, that's a really good idea. I'll just tear the entire page out and then you can read it, and I won't lose what I want to keep. I like that."

She smiled wanly and I faded away to another part of the yard to nurse my bleeding ego. I hadn't listened to her. I was less interested in conversation than I was in expressing my anger. She had offered a reasonable alternative, and I had not even heard it. The only part of the conversation I could hear was my growing resentment with her irritation about my reading habits. So I had blasted away unnecessarily, stupidly.

Banana thinking. Learned ignorance. I know that I do not know.

That day, Jeanie helped me to grab the bananas, throw off the Talking Monkey, and learn to listen.

NOTES

[1] Ronald J. Allen, Scott Black Johnston, and Barbara S. Blaisdell, *Theology for Preaching* (Nashville: Abingdon, 1997), p. 46.

[2] Richard Bach, *Illusions* (New York: Delacorte Press, 1977), p. 51.

[3] Faith Popcorn, *The Popcorn Report* (New York: Doubleday, 1991), chaps. 3 and 5.

[4] Scott Beck, cited by Penny Parker, "Boston Chicken CEO philosophical," *The Denver Post,* June 4, 1997, p. 3C.

[5] Ibid.

[6] Dag Hammarskjold, *Markings* (New York: Alfred A. Knopf, 1964), p.53.

16

Love

Once upon a time there was a frog.

But he wasn't really a frog.

He was a prince who looked and felt like a frog. A wicked witch had cast a spell on him, and only the kiss of a beautiful maiden could save him from his frogness.

But no one wanted to kiss this frog!

So there he sat—an unkissed prince in frog form.

Then one day, along came a beautiful maiden who gave this frog a great big smack.

Crash! Boom! Zap! @#!!*

There he was at last, a handsome, dashing prince.

And you know the rest of the story. They lived happily ever after.

So what is our task as human beings, Christians, and the church? To kiss frogs, of course!

Love has transforming, energizing, tranquilizing, supersizing power unlike any other power on earth or known to humankind! It is not the people who know the most, or who have the most, or who've been educated the most, but those who love the most who will change the world the most!

Unfortunately, there are many lies that are spread about today in the name of this power called love. I was about to use the word "myth." Myth, however, a legendary story that points to a larger truth, is not the right word for a discussion of love. Too much of what is written and said about love is not in any sense true.

Granted, lies and love have gone hand in hand since Cro-Magnon man first laid eyes on the woman of his dreams. She says to him, "I just love the way your craggy brow juts over your deep-set eyes. It's so...so...intelligent...so...Neanderthal!" Read: "He's dumber than a sack of hair." Today, the lies continue: She says to him, "No, I'll clean up after dinner tonight; you just rest." Read: "Instead of watching *Home Improvement* for an hour, why don't you get off your fat behind and do home improvements for an hour?" Or, he says, "Fat? Come on! If you were any skinnier we'd need heat sensitive radar just to find you!" Read: "Like, what am I supposed to say? 'Well, chubbo, you *are* getting a bit on the plump side!'"

There are five major lies embedded in conventional wisdom that have contributed to some spectacular misunderstandings and failures. Since the word "lie" is rather strong, I'll use the expression "non-truth" instead.

First Non-truth: If I Am Not in Love, My Marriage Is a Failure

The *American Heritage Dictionary* has reduced the time-honored, Platonic and neoplatonic notions of love with which Western civilization has been enamored for over two millennia to nothing more than sex and sports! It defines love as "an intense affection and warm feeling for another person; strong sexual desire for another person; a strong fondness or enthusiasm; or a zero score in tennis."

Sex and sports. That's the denotative meaning of the word. No wonder that when we do fall in lust, most describe it as the most exquisite and indescribable feeling ever. Anna Quindlen, writing for the *New York Times*, recalls it as "entering into a state more like a tropical disease than a relationship." Dr. Michael Liebowitz of Columbia University explains this by suggesting that the feeling is similar to an amphetamine boost. He speculates that something physiological is happening in the brains of those who have fallen in love. The brain is probably releasing phenylethylamine, a chemical that acts as a stimulant, summoning extra energy, boosting the heart rate, and making the world look great when you are with this person. People think they are getting hooked on romance when it is possible they are getting high on drugs, a specific drug that is flooding their brains.[1] Liebowitz's theory also accounts for the "falling-out-of-love" phenomenon. The crash has a lot to do, he says, with drug withdrawal. The brain can release phenylethylamine for only so long. When the supply is exhausted, the love rush disappears and the victim wonders, "How did I get into this?!"

Medieval physicians were on the same track. When an individual or individuals were found to be in a lovestruck situation, they were thought literally to be "lovesick," and there was a complete pathology developed to address the problem. In the eleventh-century document, the *Liber de heros morbo*, a North African physician describes the symptoms of the disease of love: "Their eyes are necessarily hollow and rapidly moving because of thoughts of...the beloved; there is a great desire to smile. Their eyelids are swollen, their skin yellow from the admixture of red bile generated by excessive wakefulness; their pulse is strong without a natural [beat]."

A complicated and extensive remedy for such an affliction was prescribed: "Drinking wine, music, and talking with friends—take place in gardens and meadows with flowing water, everything is altogether more delightful. But if gardens or meadows are lacking, let some delightful rooms be well strewn with flowers, roses, willow branches, myrtle, and basil. Intoxication should be avoided and brief naps are desirable. Afterward the patients should take pleasure in baths with temperate and clear air and water. Nor should anything approach them that might cause revulsion."[2]

From this medieval tradition of courtly love and the nature of such love and its concomitant symptoms of disease have come our Western notions of love and what it means to be "in love." Today, we expect those who say they are in love to also display the symptoms of "lovesickness." Because the endorphin rush of being in love is such a high, we plausibly assume that married life with our beloved should perpetuate these very same emotions.

The lies continue in the wedding ceremony itself. George Bernard Shaw cynically observed:

When two people are under the influence of the most violent, most insane, most delusive, and most transient of passions, they are required to swear that they will remain in that excited, abnormal and exhausting condition until death do them part.[3]

Of course, within a fortnight of the marriage, they are quarreling about his socks and underwear in a heap on the floor in the corner and her time preening in the bathroom. The sheen is off the matrimonial varnish, and despair often begins to insinuate itself into the pores and cracks of the veneer. Too often a condition then develops that led Gloria Steinem on one occasion to observe that "The surest way to be alone is to get married."

Compounding the problem are excessively high and unreasonable expectations. When he marries her, he expects her to always be thin and beautiful. What he gets is a light eater—as soon as it gets light, she starts eating. He expects someone who hates maxing the credit cards. What he gets is a woman who comes home from the mall shouting, "Veni, vidi, visa!" (I came, I saw, I charged). He expects someone who will be supportive and encouraging. What he gets is someone who reminds him that he has only two faults: everything he says and everything he does.

She, on the other hand, marries him and expects that he will be a scintillating conversationalist and raconteur. What she gets are occasional flashes of silence that make his conversation brilliant. She expects someone who will share the parenting duties and help around the house. What she gets is someone who supports her in the manner to which she is accustomed—he lets her keep her job. She expects someone who will thoughtfully allocate blocks of the weekend for romantic interludes. What she gets is someone who always takes her to the best restaurants—someday he may even take her inside. She expects someone who will work hard. What she gets is a miracle worker—it's a miracle when he works.

THE LEX OF LOVE

Agape: Selfless love driven by the welfare of the one loved.

Love: A personal experience of attraction or kinship with another person.

Limerence: The experience of utter, irrational obsession with another person even if that love is not returned.

Lovesickness: The agony of love when separated from the loved one, or when one's entreaties are met with indifference.

Falling in Love: The experience of sudden attraction and bondedness to another person, which in itself becomes a source of inexplicable and surpassing joy.

Lust: The desire for sexual gratification, which often parades in the guise of "inloveness."

The truth is that God calls us not to be in a romantic relationship fed by chemicals and unrealistic expectations, but in a loving covenant with each other. The love to which we are called has nothing to do with fuzzy feelings, hormones or glandular explosions, candlelight, wine and roses—as enjoyable and frequent as those moments may be. Rather, it has everything to do with

- supporting each other
- encouraging each other
- dreaming with each other
- sharing with each other
- laughing and crying with each other
- hugging and cuddling each other
- making love with each other
- forgiving each other
- being kind to each other
- being honest with each other
- making sacrifices for each other

When all of these qualities are totaled, they add up to a great and long-lasting love. The math of love reveals a marriage which, in the words of Barbara Defoe Whitehead, is "psychologically dynamic, requiring spouses to change over time in response to each other and also to develop the capacity to adjust to external change."[4]

Thus, Judith Wallerstein and Sandra Blakeslee argue in their book *The Good Marriage: How and Why Love Lasts* that the "challenges of marriage are essentially moral."[5] In her review of this book, Whitehead suggests that it is for this reason that Wallerstein and Blakeslee call the book *The Good Marriage* rather than *The Happy Marriage*. Marriage is essentially "a school of virtue, a domain that requires tact and restraint.…Good marriages are not free of conflict. However, the conflict is governed by a respect for the partner's deepest vulnerabilities. No matter how fierce the anger, it stops short of the cruelest cut. Spouses learn what the relationship can tolerate without breaking."[6]

This is agape love. A *good* marriage is the fruit of agape love. A *happy* marriage, as Frankl puts it, "necessarily ensues."

Still, sometimes things simply do not work right. A child is passing through a developmentally demanding phase. The children have sports commitments that take the family in every direction every weekend for months at a time. Both spouses are working at career jobs, and quality time is difficult to find.

This describes precisely the life of Brenda and Kevin and their family. They came to my office experiencing stress and a strained relationship. Their marriage was failing. They feared it was "on the rocks." After listening to them express their concerns, I said to them, "Your family is obviously dysfunctional."

They glanced at me sharply as though I had slapped them in the face. I continued, "Well, isn't it? The word dysfunctional simply means not working. Right now things are not working, correct?" They nodded silently.

I leaned forward. "I want to tell you something. Every relationship moves in and out of dysfunctionality. That is the nature of a dynamic relationship. The only relationships that do not become dysfunctional are static ones. A static relationship is a dead relationship." They started to show interest; light seemed to turn on in their eyes. "So, let's not be afraid of this word. However, we want to get rid of the dysfunction, and that requires a mid-course recalibration. Something needs to be recalibrated, changed." I cited the analogy of the Golden Gate Bridge, in a continual state of repainting without which the bridge would fall into decay and ruin. I then went on to suggest they look at possible points in their life that needed "repainting" or that could be adjusted to ease the pressure.

I tell Brenda's and Kevin's story as a reminder that what they had going for them was agape love. They had a strong sense of the narrative structure of their relationship, a sense their lives were together telling a story. They rejected the myth of the romantic marriage in favor of a quest for a good marriage. Fortunately, they saw that they already had what they were seeking.

Second Non-truth: Love Has No Bonds

For the ancient Greeks, love was a strange and wonderful thing. They had several words to describe its nature, scope, and function. Yet, whatever they thought of love, they didn't think that their gods had much of it. Of course, the gods had plenty of love for each other. Witness the stories of Zeus and his countless affairs. But the gods were remarkably cold in their feelings toward humans.

Thus, the words of the apostles Paul and John about agape love came as something of a shock to the Greek philosophical world. Both writers argue, first, that there is one God. *That's* new and different. They go on to suggest, second, that this God is not only capable of love, *but loves human beings.* Mind-boggling! And third, they offer the startling news that the love with which God loves us is agape, sacrificial, uplifting, selfless love. Indeed, God died on a cross for humans! Scandalous! (See 2 Corinthians 1.) Divine love as a model for human love is a love that is willing to suffer and pay a price.

First Corinthians 13, therefore, is a revolutionary manifesto of radical love! Love that binds, suffers, and pays a price. Here is a God who loves us, thereby binding himself in covenant with us unconditionally. Love has bonds. Kahlil Gibran writes in *The Prophet:* "Love one another, but make not a bond of love. Let it rather be a moving sea between the shores of your souls. Fill each other's cup but drink not from one cup. Give one another of your bread but eat not from the same loaf."[7] The assertion "Make not a bond of love" for Paul is a rather silly notion. Is it possible for agape love to be without commitment, without a spiritual bond? For Kahlil Gibran, living a dissolute life in New York in a small flat in Greenwich Village and surviving off the resources of his wife, not to make a bond of love seemed like a good thing.

Yet, love by its nature binds, makes a connection, to the thing loved. It is patient and kind; it bears all things, believes, hopes, and endures. It is not into control and keeping score; it is not irritable and resentful.

This is the binding way in which God loves us. It is the way we should love one another.

Third Non-truth: Love Yourself First, Then Others

It is axiomatic these days that before we can love others, perhaps even God, we must first learn to love ourselves. Malcolm Boyd, for example, offers seven suggestions in his article "How to Love Another Person." The first point he makes is that "we must be able to love ourselves first before we can love another person."[8]

This is a false and pernicious idea that we ought to abandon, and the sooner the better.

Of course, I don't mean to suggest that the proper attitude toward one's self is hatred or loathing. Such an attitude does not honor our personhood, and the dignity with which God has endowed us. Nor do I suggest that there are not those who should properly give some attention to how they value themselves and how they esteem themselves.

Yet, having said that—there is something so very middle class and Eurocentric about this preoccupation with self that bothers me. In a world in which so few people have the luxury of taking daily stock of their self-esteem, the question of my self-love seems trite and fundamentally inconsiderate. The streets of our inner cities are teeming with so-called "super-predator" kids, the AIDS virus is killing more than 25,000 people annually in this country alone, 75 percent of the world's children are malnourished, the rain forests are continually depleted by rapacious multinational corporations. Existential angst over the health of my self-image seems grotesquely inappropriate. It also becomes an excuse for social inactivity and cultural unawareness. We consider ourselves such a major project of reconstruction that we are not able— yet—to get to the larger concerns of the world around us.

The scriptures do not teach that we should love ourselves first. Jesus is not concerned whether an act of charity comes from a person whose self-esteem is high or low. He is more concerned that a person who needs help gets help. What the Bible does say is that we should love our neighbors as ourselves. Jesus here assumes that self-love is at a fundamental level something that we all possess. None of us in our right minds would willingly take an action that is self-destructive (once we are enslaved by a destructive habit, we are unwilling participants in the behavior that destroys or damages us). No healthy person, that is, free of a major psychosis, is devoid of self-love. Therefore, in relation to our neighbors, we should love them as we love ourselves. This is another way of stating the golden rule of Jesus or the silver rule of Confucius. Do unto others (do not do to others) as you would have them (not) do to you. This is not a text that can be used to advance the doctrine of self-love—at least not as we have come to understand self-love today.

Augustine plausibly argues that we should not regard Self as the True Good, but should rather seek the true good of Self, which is God. When we seek God as the true end of Self, problems of self-esteem will vanish or diminish in importance. I cannot imagine Mother Teresa attending a seminar to work on her self-esteem.

Actually, the first person to raise this issue in scripture is Moses. God calls him for service, and the first thing Moses does is raise the self-esteem issue. Here is a guy who has been educated at the Harvard University of his day, lived in the lap of luxury, surrounded by a civilization then at the peak of its glory, and when God calls him to service he says, "God, I really don't have the self-confidence for the kind of job you are talking about. Can you get someone else?" Of course, you know the rest of the story. God reluctantly agreed to send his brother along with him, an arrangement that caused no end of trouble and confusion.

When we talk, therefore, about the need to love as a means of learning to fall and get up again, let us first assume that we have enough love for ourselves to get the job done. We will miserably fail and continue to have significant failures in our lives until we put the question of self-love and self-esteem to rest. We love ourselves plenty. Now we can get on with it.

Fourth Non-truth: A Great Love Does Great Things

Get on with what? We need to get on with a very important Greek word used in the New Testament more than in any other text in the ancient world. Paul and John are the primary voices through whom we learn about this word: *agape.*

The use of the word *agape*, as we have seen, was rather radical for its time, and when it is expressed today, it is still radical. Agape love is radical love. It leaves behind questions of self-esteem, it abandons notions of reciprocated love and instead embraces a sort of unconditional, sacrificial love that was virtually ignored then and is dismissed as impractical today. Paul's most memorable reference to this love is found in his hymn to love in 1 Corinthians 13. Here he talks about what love is not and then what love is.

Notice the priority Paul gives to this love. Love, he says, is not about being the great communicator. I can talk in the language of angels, but without love, it's a big zero. Love is also not about faith. So what if I have the faith to toss a mountain into

1 CORINTHIANS 13

If I speak in the tongues of mortals and of angels, but do not have love, I am noisy gong or a clanging cymbal...If I give away all my possessions...but do not have love, I gain nothing.

Love is patient; love is kind; love is not envious or boastful or arrogant or rude....It bears all things, believes all things, hopes all things, endures all things. Love never ends.... And now faith, hope, and love abide, these three; and the greatest of these is love.

the ocean; if I don't have agape love, I am nothing. And love is not about philanthropy or martyrdom. I can give away my fortune and/or my life, but without love, it's nada.

Paul's point? In the words of my friend, Tom Russell, love is not about doing heroic deeds.

I am not so sure I like that. I really have a fondness for the heroic, the dramatic gesture, the big scheme, the grand entrance. I would much prefer to be able to do something grand to tell my wife how much I love her—an airplane tugging a banner over Coors Field, a crescendo of fireworks, or a romantic getaway. I'd love to donate a fortune (if I had one) to build a new wing on the hospital or some such thing.

Nothing is wrong with any of the above; but let's not confuse them with love. Love is something other than balloons and fireworks. Paul explains: love is patience, endurance, trust, hope, and faith. It is not the pride of achievement; it is the poverty of pride. It is not building an impressive monument; it is breathing in a creative space. It is not sanctifying of the self; it is rather sacramentalizing the mundane. It is not being a hero, but an anti-hero. It is not the heroic doing so much as it is benevolent non-doing; not action so much as inaction. Lao Tsu foreshadows the wisdom of Paul when he says in the *Tao Te Ching*, "A truly good man is not aware of his goodness, and is therefore good. A foolish man tries to be good, and is therefore not good. A truly good man does nothing, yet leaves nothing undone. A foolish man is always doing, yet much remains to be done."[9]

In short, love is cleaning the toilet.

When we live our lives with this kind of love, who can fail? How can one possibly be considered a failure in life who knows this kind of success? It is impossible. It doesn't matter whether your self-image is suffering today, or if the self-image meter is low. If you have learned how to love in a way that seeks no glory, puts on no airs, thinks the best, endures, believes, bears all things, is patient and kind—when the falls of life come, you'll take them gently and be bouncing up again in no time. You cannot be a failure when you love with agape love.

It's possible that the world will think you a failure, but not those touched by your love.

The tragic reality is that we find this kind of love very difficult. In *The Brothers Karamazov* Dostoevsky refers to what he calls being "unable to love." Are we creating a narcissistic culture so self-absorbed that it is unable to love? Can we who live in a culture which published *Life*, then *People*, then *Us*, and now *Self*, know what it means to express agape love? Where is the magazine called *Others*?

Fifth Non-truth: Love of God Is So Much Pie-in-the-Sky

How does one go about loving God? A lot of people have trouble whipping up an emotional frenzy about God. Some people don't have any difficulty at all living in an emotional aura of love for God. That's okay, but it's not my cup of bliss. It certainly is not what Jesus meant when he said, "You shall love the Lord your God with all your soul, heart, mind, and strength." Clearly, to love God is not to *do* any one specific thing for God. God really doesn't need anything done for him, thank you very much. The words of Jesus indicate that loving God is a state of being that encompasses the whole of our existence. We love God with our souls and hearts, that is, the intuitive persons we are, and with our mind and strength, that is, the rational, volitional creatures we are. Still,

Some say they love God by going to church every Sunday.
Some say they love God by going to church every Sunday night,
Wednesday night, and days in between.
Some say they love God by pledging money to the church.
Some say they love God by not breaking the Ten
Commandments.
Some say they love God by reading the Bible every day.
Some say they love God by praying to God at least once a week.
Some say they love God by enjoying the great outdoors.
Some say they love God by expressing thanks for the blessings
of creation.
Some say they love God by doing a good deed.
Some say they love God by not swearing.
Some say they love God by living a chaste life.

I don't see it this way. For me, loving God is not work, but a walk. The prophet Micah provides the paradigm here. What does God ask of us? God asks us to walk with God. There it is. Jesus says we should love (read: walk with) God with our intuitive and rational selves.

What happens on a pleasant walk with a friend? Sharing (intuitive) and good conversation (rational). A walk is an intimate experience. To walk with someone is to express solidarity and understanding. It is a mark of friendship and camaraderie. It is a signal of intimacy.

What is the first thing God wanted to do with the first humans, according to the creation account in Genesis? God wanted to walk and converse. Earlier in the day, God meets with Adam and Eve, gives them the garden tour, goes over the job description, and then explains the house rules: "Clothing optional and free meals. Just don't mess with my tree over there and we'll get along fine." Then God adds, "Let's go for a walk tonight. Six-ish okay?" Of course, it was fine with Adam and Eve, except by evening their world had begun to unravel, and when God came in the cool of the evening for a congenial walk, those erstwhile companions were too embarrassed to appear. To love God is to walk with God.

Of course, the question begging to be asked is: "Fine. But what does it mean to walk with God?"

Fair enough. The prophet Micah says that we should walk with God humbly, do justice, and love kindness. That is to say, the whole of our intuitive and rational life is to be acted out as those who are in deep fellowship and communion with the eternal God. The question then becomes, are my attitude and my behavior an expression of humility, justice, and kindness, that is, love? *Excuse me, God, while I respond to the jerk driving in the next lane. Excuse me, God, while I neglect my family. Excuse me, God, while I betray the trust placed in me. Excuse me, God, while I berate this employee. Excuse me, God, while I am rude to the check-out girl at Safeway. Thank you. Now then, what were you saying, God?*

Do you see now why love is such an important component in learning to fall? If I fall while in the love of God, it sure isn't much of a fall. When you fall, it can't hurt your pride because you're walking humbly with God. It can't break your spirit because walking with God inspires hope. A fall can rob you of your time, money, and possessions. But those are things that we shall all lose someday; it's just a question of when. Jesus advises us to die early, as we have observed elsewhere. If we deny ourselves and take up our cross, then falling sort of loses the power to frighten us, doesn't it?

Sixth Non-truth: Your Neighbors Are the Poor and Needy, the Downtrodden and Oppressed, the Marginalized and Outcasts of Society.

Wrong. Your neighbor is the person who lives next door or who is in your field of vision at any given time.

Granted, Jesus taught the story of the good Samaritan as a lesson in neighborliness. But notice that Jesus does not make the point that the righteous in Jerusalem should organize a mission trip to the needy in Samaria. He does not suggest that the youth group should rent five buses and caravan to Jericho for a ministry to the lepers. His point is that neighbors are not just those of "our kind" but rather any person of any race, religion, sex, or state of mental and physical health in our line of vision who needs our help.

What about those who live in the projects who don't have any good Samaritan, neighborly types in their line of vision? Who will be neighbors to them? Good point. Injustice must be resisted, and the unfortunate must be helped. There is plenty of biblical warrant for such actions.

Too often, however, we overlook the person next door while trying to do justice under the "good neighbor policy" Jesus talked about. The poor are not our neighbors; they are the poor, and they need our help. Helping the poor is a biblical imperative; it is a no-brainer. The prophets speak loud and clear about this obligation. I am drawing a distinction here, however, between the biblical "neighbor" and the biblical "stranger" or "alien" whom we are also told to befriend and help. But befriending the "stranger" or "alien" is not the lesson of the good Samaritan, nor is this what Jesus meant when he said we should "love our neighbors as ourselves." (All the more so because it is the "alien," i.e., the Samaritan, who renders the good deed to the Jew.) He really meant our "neighbor," the person next door, the person in our pathway.

Our neighbor is the guy who lives next door, laid up with emphysema, who can't get to the doctor's office. Our neighbor is the single parent two houses away who can't get day care for the infant child. Our neighbor is the guy on the south of us whose dog poops on our lawn every day. Our neighbor is the family down the street that just moved in. These are our neighbors, and if you are like most Americans, you don't know the names of these people.

What an expression of simple and profound love to begin the process of creating a friendship. Although the motivation is love, the result is what I call "fall insurance." When you spend a lifetime loving, you are loved. What a soft fall it is when the discouragements of life are cushioned by those whose falls we have helped to cushion. When we bear burdens, our burdens are borne.

Want to fall without breaking something important?

Forgive

Apologize

Learn

Love!

NOTES

[1]Cited by Anastasia Toufexis, "Love: The Right Chemistry," *The St Martin's Guide to Writing*, Rise B. Axelrod and Charles R. Cooper, eds. (New York: St. Martin's Press, 1994), p. 167.

[2]See Mary Frances Wack, "The *Liber de heros morbo* of Johannes Afflacius and Its Implcations for Medieval Love Conventions," *Speculum* 62:2 (1987), p. 324ff.

[3]Source untraced.

[4]Barbara Dafoe Whitehead, "The Moral State of Marriage," *The Atlantic Monthly*, September 1995, pp. 117–118.

[5]Cited by Whitehead, ibid., p. 118.

[6]Ibid., p. 118–119.

[7]Kahlil Gibran, "On Marriage," *The Prophet* (New York: Alfred A. Knopf, 1963), p. 15.

[8]Malcolm Boyd, "How to Love Another Person," *Modern Maturity*, July/August, 1995, p. 84.

[9]*Tao Te Ching*, p. 38.

IV

Observations
from the
Chair Lift

17

It Wouldn't Hurt to Take a Few Lessons

There is an ancient Greek legend that when the gods made the human species, they fell to arguing as to where to put the answers to life so the humans would have to search for them. One god said, "Let's put the answers on top of a mountain. They will never look for them there." The others said, "No, they will find them right away."

Another of the gods said, "Let's put them in the center of the earth. They will never look for them there." But the others said that they would find them with no trouble at all.

Still another god spoke up, "Let's put the answers to life at the bottom of the sea. They will never look for them there." But the others said that the humans would surely find them at the bottom of the sea.

Finally, another god suggested, "We can put the answers to life within them. They will never look for them there."

And so they did.

Jesus said, "The kingdom of God is within you." While he also spoke of the kingdom of God as a future reality, his emphasis on the kingdom of God as an inner, spiritual reality confused his listeners. They wondered, "How can there be a kingdom within us?"

On one occasion, Jesus spoke of a man who went away to "receive a kingdom." When this man went to get the kingdom, what precisely do you think he got? A map? A clod of dirt that he carried back with him? What he received was the *authority* to rule.

Jesus' point is clear. God's authority to rule in our lives is within us. The secret to the presence of God in every moment of every day lies within the deep spaces and yawning openness of our lives. When we think to look there—inside—we will find the voice of God ready to order our lives in a way that redeems the falls we experience and sets our feet on solid ground.

Of course, we all think we can recognize the still, small voice of God when we hear it, don't we? How interesting it is, however, to realize that for most of us, God speaks in English and is a member of our own particular denomination or spiritual affiliation! The idea that perhaps God speaks a multitude of languages and need not be an old, white male of our ecclesiastical bearing is a bit radical!

I remember when I was a young minister attending committee meetings at the Annual Conference. I sat in on many discussions as to which speakers to invite to the conference for the following year. Consistently, the top brass invited speakers within our own denomination. I wasn't always impressed. I urged them to consider resources beyond our narrow perspective. But it never happened. I always thought we were impoverished by such a policy. Not to listen to voices outside of our tradition and language severely limits our take on life.

To really be good at something we take lessons from the masters, from those who have excelled. The religions and philosophies of the world have, in part, the goal to understand humankind's place in the universe and the meaning of that place.

Scandalous idea—that Christians could profit by taking lessons from other religions!

Justin, the Martyr (d. 160), became a Christian only after visiting a variety of philosophical schools (as Augustine did later). He found in Christianity, however, the surest path to the truth. He believed that the divine Logos was an active principle that had been at work in the universe even before time and had inspired and enlightened the philosophers of the world of whom he held Socrates and Heraclitus in especial esteem. Then in the Old Testament he saw the record of the faithful Abraham. The Logos most perfectly appeared in Jesus. Thus, Justin established a rationale for appropriating the light that non-Christian thinkers have and utilizing that light to guide our pathway.

Christianity, of course, is central to our theme, for it deals specifically with the notion of falling. The "fall" has been a theological paradigm of the church for two millennia. However, scripture is a record not only of the fall, but also of God's response to the fall, the appearance of God in Jesus Christ bringing redemption to humankind. Redeeming the fall is at the heart of the good news of Christianity. But I have benefited from other "takes" on the human experience. Hinduism, for example, reminds me that a variety of choices lie before human beings, just as Christians remember the choice that faced Adam and Eve in the Genesis story of the first human moral conflict. Hinduism describes two paths that humans can take divided into two paths each: (1) the path of desire, or (2) the path of renunciation. The path of desire is a two-fold path of pleasure and worldly success. This is a perfectly legitimate choice to make if this is what we want. But if we walk this path, we must be prepared to face the dangers along the way. The pathway of desire is competitive and precarious; its goals, being materialistic, are empty and vapid; the achievements along the way are ephemeral. In time, many people, having started on the path of desire, turn to another path, the pathway of renunciation. They now renounce their former direction, and walk instead on the two-fold path of duty and liberation. Walking on this path brings liberation from the limitations that beset us. Freedom from these limitations can be achieved through yoga disciplines of knowledge (jnana yoga), love (bhakti yoga), work (karma yoga), and discipline (raja yoga).

The word *desire* is a common word that appears in many of the writings of the religions of the world. Clearly, the human experience is a story of struggling with human desire that more often than not leads us in directions where we really don't want to go. Paul articulated this in his famous burst of frustration in his letter to the Romans: "The good I want to do, I don't; and the bad I don't want to do, I do!" Buddhism, indeed, attributes human suffering to the root cause of desire *(tanha)*. But there is hope, for one can overcome desire (and thus suffering) by embarking on a pilgrimage along the eightfold path: right knowledge, right aspiration, right speech, right behavior, right livelihood, right effort, right mindfulness, and right absorption. This program of overcoming desire is a sort of "treatment by training," based on the conviction that good health is contagious. It calls for intentional living to overcome the sources of discomfort and suffering. These sources can be found in improper desire which, if removed, can remove the suffering itself. Thus, if I am unhappy because I am not making enough money, it must be because I desire things that my present income cannot afford. Therefore, if I can remove this want, if I can learn to want what I already have, the suffering will cease when the desire is gone. This concept is not far removed from the apostle Paul's witness to the Christians at Philippi: "I have learned whatever state I am in therewith to be content."

The Sufi masters of Islam identify pride as the most basic conundrum of the human experience. It is pride that separates humans from God. It stems from the pleasure we take in our own accomplishments, especially when these accomplishments earn the praise of others. To combat pride, Sufis developed a practice of self-reproach *(malamat)*; severely disciplined life-style *(zuhd)*; remembrance *(dhikr),* which consists of mental or verbal repetition of the names of God or a verse of the Koran; prayer *(tahajjud),* which was practiced in the early hours of the morning, shortly after midnight, following the habit of Mohammed; and suffering, as a means of divorcing oneself from all that is not God.

While I'm not about to get up at midnight to pray, the Sufi notion of pride as not only a formidable obstacle to spiritual growth but the active cause of the poverty of the human spirit is an attractive one. It echoes the Judeo-Christian emphasis on the forgetting of self in order to embrace a force beyond oneself. "Deny yourself," Jesus said. "Take up your cross," he said. The Hebrew prophets and writers consistently warned of the dangers of pride.

With the Sufi masters, I will stop. However, Taoism, Confucianism, and Zoroastrianism (to which Judaism, Christianity, and Islam owe much) are also worthy of thoughtful reading.

Reading

Some have argued that the invention of the printing press in the late fifteenth century made the Reformation of Martin Luther and his colleagues possible. The next hundred years experienced an explosion in knowledge as presses churned out incunabula and books at an unprecedented rate.

Today, with advances in computer technology, publishing and writing have been taken to a new level. White Europeans no longer are limited to the admittedly great literary tradition of the past 600 years but are now able to read and listen to brilliant contemporary voices who are sharing both their history and ideas. Even though this history and these ideas may sound strange to our ears and may not come from within a specifically "Christian" tradition, they are worthy of consideration. Here are a few of my favorites.

Hisaye Yamamoto was born in California of Japanese immigrants, but during World War II she was interned with thousands of other Japanese Americans in a relocation camp. Her writing reflects both this experience and the strong cultural heritage provided by her parents. The winner of numerous awards, her stories can be found in *Seventeen Syllables and Other Stories* (1989) as well as other works.

There are many African-American authors who have commented on the American experience. Richard Wright, James Baldwin, Alice Walker, Toni Cade Bambara, Chinu Achebe, and Bell Hooks are some I read regularly.

Sandra Cisneros grew up as a "poor Latina" in a ghetto neighborhood in Chicago. She didn't think of herself as a Chicana writer until she participated in a writer's workshop while working on her master's degree at the University of Iowa. Some of her stories can be found in *The House on Mango Street* (1983) and *Woman Hollering Creek and Other Stories* (1991). Jorge Luis Borges (1899–1986), the Argentinean writer of fiction, began his literary career in an avant-garde literary movement known as ultraisme, an outgrowth of expressionism in which metaphor and figure were exaggerated so as to become larger and more important than plot. I mention him here because he influenced an entire generation of postmodernist writers. His work includes *Fictions* (1944), *Labyrinths* (1962), *The Aleph and Other Stories* (1972) and others.

Saadat Hasan Manto (1912–1955) has been described by Salmon Rushdie as "the undisputed master of the modern Indian short story." Born in the Indian state of Punjab, he was forced to migrate to Pakistan after the partitioning of India in 1947. He comments on the turmoil of this period: "Thousands of Hindus and Muslims were dying all around us. Why were they dying? All these questions had different answers: the Indian answer, the Pakistani answer, the British answer. Every question had an answer, but when you tried to look for truth, they were no help."

He died at age forty-two of alcoholism. He wrote his own epitaph: "Here lies Saadat Hasan Manto. With him lie buried all the arts and mysteries of short story writing. Under tons of earth he lies, wondering if he is a greater short story writer than God." He wrote over 200 short stories. Some of them can be found in *Kingdom's End and Other Stories* (1987).

Another Indian-born writer to explore is Bharati Mukherjee. Born in Calcutta, Mukherjee has written novels (*The Tiger's Daughter,* 1972; *Wife*, 1975) as well as short stories (*The Middleman and Other Stories*, 1988).

Es'kia Mphahlele was born in Pretoria, South Africa, writes about the experience of black Africans in South Africa, and takes his readers into the lives of those who live in the slums of Soweto or the lives of the township dwellers. Two collections of his short stories are *The Living and the Dead* (1961) and *In Corner B* (1967).

This list is, of course, a vastly abbreviated list of writers outside the Eurocentric literary tradition. But for those who are interested in taking lessons on falling and getting up again and are willing to step outside their traditional comfort zone, it is a place to start.

18

Dances with Trees

And you knew who you were then,
girls were girls, and men were men.

—Theme song from *All in the Family*

Part of my fear of falling is gender related. I am a guy, and guys generally hate to fail.

When my family and I were traveling in Israel, we rented a car in Jerusalem and drove it north through the West Bank on our way to Nazareth. Some of the cities of the West Bank were just then being turned over to the Palestinian Authority. Evidence of political tension and social unrest was everywhere. The rental agency did not want to rent us the car because we were staying in Bethlehem at the Tantur Ecumenical Institute, a West Bank address.

After persuading them to rent us a car we drove north through Ramallah and Nablus. I was conscious of the need to allay whatever fears my family might have about our safety—fears that could be exacerbated by getting lost! So I consulted the map frequently and on two occasions even stopped to ask directions! Hey, what a guy!

Later in the day, as we were driving out of Nazareth looking for the highway to take us to Tiberius, my wife turned toward me and said, "Honey, I want to thank you for listening to the feminine side of your nature."

I took that in silence for a few moments. The problem with listening to the feminine side of my nature is that it slows me down. It makes me tentative and unsure of myself. I am confident that the direction and route we are taking are the right ones, but stopping to ask questions and consulting the map all take time. And then, even when I am simply making a routine left turn, I hesitate, wondering if this is the right way.

I explained this to my wife, and then said, "Honey, would it be okay if, for the rest of the afternoon, we just let the testosterone kick in and go for it?"

She smiled and nodded. I shifted down, put the pedal to the metal, and we roared off to Tiberius, getting there in record time. (Records are also very important.)

I have always had this problem—the problem of listening too much to the feminine side of my nature. Not too long ago, influenced by Robert Bly, author of *Iron John: A Book About Men,* I decided to do something about it.

Bly argues that the first step to understanding ourselves as men is to recover our manliness. My problem is that I'm too sensitive and too nurturing and too caring. I live in a world of soft males who have discovered their feminine side. But, says Bly, I am disenchanted. The core of my male identity is not feminine. I have wandered from the essence of manhood. I need to recover the "wild man, the iron man, the fierce one," which is the true psychic core of my being.

Being a wild man intrigues me. But I've always thought that men were the *agents* of cultural oppression, not the *victims* of it. Herb Goldberg, a best-selling author and clinical psychologist in Los Angeles, disagrees: "Men are the true victims of gender because they are living 10 years less than women. They have higher rates of all disease and are killing themselves more often."[1]

I thought I should look into this. Some time off for holistic enhancement would be helpful. After talking to my wife about it, I proposed to take a mythopoetic journey into the hills above Boulder, Colorado, to engage in the ritual of masculine self-discovery. If I couldn't discover myself in Boulder, the city identified by Sunday Magazine of the *New York Times* as a hotbed of virtual reality, then such discovery wasn't possible—at least not for me.

I met Craig, a pharmacist from Denver and one of the leaders of the Boulder Men's Council. He suggested a possible agenda for the weekend that included a variety of liturgical rituals drawn from ancient Indian folklore. We started with a trek into a deep ravine, where we found a cache of gray, cinder-flecked ashes. These ashes symbolized all the old emotional issues I hadn't faced. "We are like stoves when we're young," Craig said knowingly. "We put a lot of stuff into the stove and if we never take out the ashes and carry them away, we don't work very well." I remembered, as a small boy in Regina, Saskatchewan, carrying out the cinders of the old coal furnance. This made a lot of sense to me. I quickly stepped over the pile of ashes—thereby cleaning out my emotional stove.

The recalibration of my male psyche was only beginning. Back at the compound, I walked through a black tapestry symbolizing my repressed self. A red tapestry awaited that signified my true warrior self. Later, as I crawled nude on all fours into a sweat lodge behind another male ambulating similarly, I understood how important it was not to feel the least bit repressed. It was then, as I was face-to-buttocks with the overweight, grunting man ahead of me, that I realized for the first time how mythopoetic this adventure was going to be

Warrior Tim…Wild Man Timothy…Timothy the Fierce One.

The sweat lodge was…sweaty…and dark. We sat au naturel with our legs drawn to our chins—about twenty of us. I did a lot of primal screaming and guttural groaning—mainly because my wig of shredded bark was driving me crazy, but also on account of the one or two men who were releasing more than their inhibitions. One man experiencing flatulence in a crowded sweat lodge creates a breezy ambiance best described as primitive; two or more doing the same thing is downright antediluvian. I felt like an animal in an ark full of Noahs.

I did make friends, however. I met Wortham, a deejay from a local classical station. Wortham had prodigious lungs. He could hold a scream louder and longer than Whitney Houston on the high C of the "Star Spangled Banner." When he accidentally sat on my spear, his vocal range made Whitney's high notes sound like Arnold Schwarzenegger on a cold morning.

Wortham and I were both given a *didjeridu*, an Australian wood flute. I looked at it in wonder. "This thing will summon Crocodile

Dundee quicker than you can say 'Tasmanian Devil,'" I thought. "Need a bit-o-help, there, eh mate?" he'd say, flicking a wedge of alligator meat out of his teeth with his Bowie knife. And I, the wild one, would snarl meaningfully and shake a gourd rattle.

That night, clad in loincloths and masks, Wortham and I danced around a pine tree while pounding on a drum. Then we were given some sticks to beat and bells to toll. That was before going down to the fire pit for some more dancing with trees and moaning with spears.I did all of this because rituals "release energy and inhibitions, thereby creating a sacred space where it's safe to share the world of male fear, feelings, and fallacies." In this safe, sacred space, I commenced the journey of discovery; my other identities as King, Warrior, Lover, Trickster, Mythologist, Cook, and the Grief Man began to emerge. Still, I wondered if it wouldn't have been easier to stay home, have a couple of beers with the guys, and watch the Broncos.

Theology always intrudes. Was I lapsing into syncretism? Departing from the historical mainstream? You bet I was. But perhaps there were some theological underpinnings—christologically weak to be sure—that could be discovered in all of this. I imagined what it might be like to sit in the rarefied atmosphere of a sweat lodge with the likes of famous theologians of the past and present: Hans Kung, for example, arguing that men are going through a *paradigm shift*, while John B. Cobb, Jr., insists on describing it as a merely *panentheistic process.* I imagine Rudolph Bultmann gloriously remythologizing the whole experience; Leonardo Boff applies the Marxist doctrine of *secular redemption* and feels happily liberated by it all. And Michael Fox, the defrocked Dominican priest, thinks he's discovered the fount of original blessing.

Thinking of Michael cavorting in a mask and loincloth, I realized why it is so hard to talk about God. There's very little transcendence in a sweat lodge. Our imannentist bodies seem firmly anchored to the earthly and fleshly. Wortham and I could talk about lawyering and doctoring and classical music, but theologizing requires clothing to do well because clothes create the illusion of upward ontological mobility. Thus the importance of ritualistically shedding garments in the men's movement that, by definition, is a return to primal origins; a step back, or down—indeed, a search for the *bottom* of the Dionysian Ladder.

As for me, I regard David as the biblical model. He's the perfect example of a 'nineties, postmodern male. He blends the nurturing, caring man with a powerfully competitive one; he's at once a Wild Man and a Sensitive Guy. Consider the Warrior David who's tearing lions limb from limb, bonking bears, slaying giants, and mutilating Philistines. Da Bearss, da lionss, da giantss, he says. Da foreskinss.

Then consider the Shepherd David who's crooning love songs, playing a lyre, and writing poetry.

So when I asked my wife in Nazareth if I could forget the feminine side and really start driving, she understood. I need to recover occasionally the core of my masculine identity. "Go for it," she said, smiling lovingly at her Wild Man.

Timothy Dances with Trees. Timothy-out-of-His-Tree.

NOTE

[1]Source untraced.

19

Shopping for a Prom Dress

New York City. Macy's Department Store. Fourth floor—Women's Apparel. I am standing forlorn amid mini-skirted mannequins and racks of skirts, blouses, and unmentionables.

Saleswomen glance my way, but I avoid looking at them. Actually, I'm here against my will: shopping with my daughter for the world's most awesome prom dress.

Danielle had asked this morning: "Why don't you come shopping with me, Dad?" Now it sounds like an eminently reasonable request, but you haven't been shopping with my daughter. I'd rather have a root canal. But I say, "Sure." So here I am.

My little girl, about to graduate from high school, has just disappeared into the nether regions of the dressing rooms. Standing guard is a fierce woman ready to chase away perverts without and laggards within. I wonder if I will ever see Danielle again.

Not to worry. Here she is in front of the full-length, five-way mirror trying on a dress. Standing sideways, she turns her head to cast a critical eye over every line, curve, and seam. She sucks in and tucks in, pinches and pulls, tugs down, and pushes up. Now frontways, now backways, rotating her head grotesquely to judge the view from behind.

One black, three pink, and two blue dresses later, I await the result. "Dad," she says breathlessly, "I need another dress." And she sends me across the aisle in search of yet another creation and this time in a different size.

Now I am sitting again and watching. One lady who has been observing this ritual thinks I am a wonderful dad. I think so, too. I begin to think back over the years to when this all-knowing teenager was not so omniscient, to when she was so little I could hold her in one hand.

I had always wanted a baby girl first. I wanted a son, to be sure, but a girl first. I dreamed about what this child would be like as she grew older, how she'd turn out, what she'd look like as an adolescent.

I planned all the fun things she and I would do together, like hiking, camping, playing softball, going to football games, and lots of girl stuff like that. And shopping. Of course, I would go shopping with my daughter.

Naturally, I did not know whereof I spoke. But in those moments when the child was young, I romanticized every detail of my life with her—even the ordinary and routine. Sacramentalizing the mundane, French priest and author Teilhard de Chardin calls it.

Now, sitting on the fourth floor of Macy's, I realize I am fulfilling a dream I'd had eighteen years earlier. I am her dad, she needs me, and I am helping her find the world's most awesome dress for the senior prom.

As I watch her, I wonder how many dreams go unfulfilled because I fail to recognize them when they appear for fulfillment. I wonder how many mistakes I've made, how many falls I've endured, how many times I've failed her and myself because I haven't been paying attention.

Danielle has reappeared and is asking me which one I like best, the black one with the puffy sleeves or the pink one with the neckline that plunges to South America.

"The black one," I say approvingly.

She bought the pink one.

20

Stumps and Stress

Stress. You have your method or methods of dealing with stress and I have mine. Some people clean and start throwing away stuff. Nothing is sacrosanct. Diving into the basement or garage, they don't come up for air until every nook, cranny, and closet has been molested. Out goes the old pole lamp, tennis shoes, clothes, vases, magazines, newspapers, paint cans, the kitchen sink, the baby *and* the bathwater, and more.

In the postmodern world of the second millennium, the Cartesian dictum "I think, therefore I am" has been changed to "I shop, therefore I am." As a stress reliever, shopping is hard to beat. We grab the credit card and hit the mall. Six hours later we come home exclaiming, "We'd better take out an equity loan on the house!"

I prefer to do something physical, getting as far away from pastoral concerns as possible: Let me run, build, tear down, garden, trim, what have you, and I'm happy. That's why we don't have any cherry trees in our back yard. I cut them all down. Felt good.

Unfortunately, the unsightly stumps remained. Cutting down five trees took about five minutes. Taking out the stump took about five weeks. Not five stumps; one stump. First a shovel and a nice ring around the stump a few inches deep. Then an ax to the larger roots and some nippers to cut at the small ones. A saw is used to carve out more working area, and then a mattock to dig deeper. I am on my hands and knees scooping the earth out, fingering between the roots, and loosening the soil. Clods fly in my face when a severed root springs back unexpectedly. Soil rolls into my trousers and jostles uninvited into my shoes.

Angles are difficult when working on a stump. One reaches, stretches, bending the back and legs. Every labor produces a groan. The chest constricts, the lungs heave with the exertion, the heart kicks into overdrive, and sweat pours over the brow.

"Are you still working on that stump?" little Alex asks blandly. He dodges the clod I toss at him.

My wife has already put in a call to the tree surgeons. Only eighty dollars to have all the stumps removed, dear, and they'll do it right away, she says to me.

I grind my teeth. "I'll take care of the stump," I say.

It came out today. The triumph of stubbornness over common sense. I had felt it weakening. I clambered into the hole, back against the wall, legs up and feet against the stump. Adrenaline surge. The legs pump, the stump falls awkwardly on its side, its roots hanging limply like spaghetti from a fork. I stand and lift it out with Schwartzeneggerian strength. Eighty dollars indeed!

Some roots are more difficult to extract. Not backyard roots, but the vines that twist and choke the heart.

The roots of intolerance. Traditions of racism and injustice. Destructive habits and patterns. An unwillingness to forgive, or the inability to take responsibility. A "root of bitterness springs up and causes trouble" (Hebrews 12:15). The tree may be cut down, but the stump and roots remain. It's unsightly and in the way. There's still work to be done.

Such work requires the sharp instruments of discipline, courage, confrontation, and faith. Instruments that are sometimes cumbersome, heavy, and hard to lift. The spirit flags, the will weakens; the roots tap deeper and twist tighter like a tourniquet around the heart until our very humanness is gone.

Yet, God is present. Little Alex, 3, assisted me in the project mentioned above by placing his chubby hands on the shaft of the shovel. My hands and arms provided the strength, my foot on the blade exerted the power, but Alex was a full partner nonetheless. "Therefore, lift your drooping hands and strengthen your weak knees," the writer to the Hebrews continues. God will provide the shovel; God will provide the power.

But God does expect us to get in there and get dirty.

21

Please Don't Show Me Your Scar

Pietro Giovanni Monza is an Italian American member of the church I recently pastored—and a survivor of quintuple bypass surgery. He loved it when on Sunday mornings I would raise my arms to salute and embrace him, exclaiming in a fake and corny Italian accent: "Bon journo, Peitro Giovanni Monza! Rigatoni, manicotti." Those were the only Italian words I could ever remember. Peter is our resident Italian chef. Whenever we have a spaghetti dinner, Peter dons an apron and whips out the secret family recipe for spaghetti sauce inherited from his grandmother in Tuscany.

I was with Peter when he was in the hospital for his last surgery. The day after surgery he was still groggy, but two days later he was remarkably chipper. On the third day, he was moved out of the cardiac care unit and to another wing in the hospital. Now we would have a chance to chat.

It wasn't long before the inevitable happened. "The docs really cut me up," Peter said. The heart monitor was disconnected now, and the IVs had been taken out.

"I'll bet they did," I said, knowing where this was leading.

"It's amazing how they can open you up and close you up—just like that." He snapped his fingers, smiling.

"Yeah."

Peter tugged at his hospital gown. "Here, let me show you." And he threw off his robe to reveal the staples in his chest tattooed there like the lacing of a football.

I winced. I knew this would happen! I don't need to see this. I don't want to see this. My mind raced over other unsightly scars to which, incredibly, I had been exposed. Knee replacement scars, hernia scars, abdominal surgeries, appendectomies, kidney removal, colostomy bags. The embarrassment is even more palpable if it's a female member of the church who insists I view the doctor's handiwork. And I, a guy who's never spent a night in the hospital in his life and doesn't particularly enjoy being in hospitals, am compelled to listen to the most amazing medical histories and see some really disgusting stuff.

While chatting with Peter, I had an insight into why my "patients" have a need to show me their scars. They are, after all, accustomed to showing me their scars, their *soul scars*. And I am, after all, their soul doctor. It's only a slight leap from baring their souls to baring their flesh, to show me where they are now physically hurting.

Hadn't the doctor asked Peter, "Where does it hurt?" And hadn't I asked Peter the night before his operation, "Where does it hurt?" Peter told me. He said he was afraid. He told me how he had spent the previous three weeks tying up the loose ends of his affairs. He told me that his son had flown in from Chicago. He told me that as far as he knew he and God had no ongoing quarrel. But he was afraid and nervous. There was pain in his soul.

As the soul doctor for my congregation, it's my calling to know where they are spiritually and emotionally in pain and to realize that often this type of pain is deeper and less amenable to remedy than physical pain.

I decided that I need to be willing to let the people of my church show me their scars. All of them. No matter how gross or ugly. That's what I am here for. They need someone who will look with compassion upon the scars of their life, who will know and understand their hurts and the deep aches and pains of their souls. They need someone with whom they can share their failings, their fallings, their risings and up-risings!

"They take a single, long piece of vein from the leg," Peter was saying. "They used to take several short sections, you know. Now, they start at the calf and go all the way up the inner thigh." He fumbled at his gown.

"Here, let me show you."

"Sure, Peter, show me," I said.

22

Sand in the Armor

If you are a medieval lord charged with the defense of the city that is now under siege, what do you do? Of course, you have your archers on the perimeter of the walls. You also have every able-bodied person on the ramparts assigned to piles of stones that will be hurled down upon the heads of the villains climbing the ladders they've leaned against your walls.

The pièce de résistance you save as the last and most terrifying resort. The fires are burning. Over them are cauldrons of oil. Workers stir into this molten mass a mix of sand and gravel. Buckets of this stuff, Greek fire, are distributed along the battlements. Should an armored warrior succeed in dodging arrows or defending himself against a hailstorm of stones and make it close to the top of the walls, a bucket of this hot oil and sand will be poured upon his head, and from there it will seep and ooze down his body and inside his armor, causing excruciating pain and discomfort. The attacker is instantly rendered immobile and is out of the game.

It's Tuesday morning, and I'm sitting in my office decidedly uncomfortable. Sand in my armor. Irritations. Frustrations. Vexations. Sometimes it feels as if the congregation I serve has been heaping coals

150

of fire on my head, and it's not the "repaying-evil-with-good" kind of fire, that Paul discusses in his letter to the Romans, either. Last Sunday Deacon Hanson complained about the inclusive version of the doxology we sing, while Mabel Bower made it a point of suggesting an alternate version of the Lord's Prayer. Our absent-minded dolt of an organist missed the cue for the choral benediction—again—and on Saturday at the wedding he let the bride walk down the aisle in total silence! The sermon was a half-hearted effort. The microphone went dead in the middle of it, and two mothers allowed their babies to holler through the whole thing. Tonight the budget committee meets to discuss another depressing financial report.

I may as well crawl off under a juniper tree like Elijah and wait for God to send an angel to encourage me. I'd do it, but the sand in my armor is driving me crazy. "I have had enough, LORD," the prophet lamented (1 Kings 19:4, NIV). Ha! He shoulda been stuck with our organist. Then he'd know what real pain is all about. Sure, he had to deal with Ahab! But he never had to squeeze a few dollars out of the trustees for new carpeting in the fellowship hall. Sure, he had Jezebel to worry about. Piece of cake! He never had to face an enraged Agnes Conway charging in with the Inclusive Language Lectionary, intending to create mischief and mayhem. What did Elijah know about being a pastor anyway?

Now that I'm beginning to recall some of the details of his story, I wish I hadn't started this train of thought. Elijah high-tailed it out of the desert and holed up in a cave on a mountain. There the wind blew, the earth shook, and a fire raged. Then he heard the voice of God coming to him as a "gentle whisper."

"Why are you here?" God says to him. It's always good to be reminded of our mission, I guess. I might've responded the same way Elijah did.

"I have been very zealous for the LORD God Almighty." (Read: I've been working my tail off for you and where have you been?)

"The Israelites have rejected your covenant, broken down your altars, and put your prophets to death with the sword." (Read: My congregation doesn't listen to a thing I say. They are throwing out the old traditions and driving good people away.)

"I am the only one left and now they are trying to kill me too" (1 Kings 19:14, NIV). (Read: I'm dying here.)

God hears this complaint and immediately calls for a reality check. "Get back to work, and by the way, anoint your successor."

"Anoint my successor? Is this any way to handle burnout? What happened to that angel out in the desert? That worked. I can live with angels helping me get the sand out of my armor and the kinks out of my attitude."

God says, "No, no. You're right. You're burned out. The embers are cold. You don't even know what you're doing and why you're here. You come to me with this lame and sorry excuse about being the only one left who is living the covenant life. Get real! It's time to wrap it up and turn things over to the new guy."

"New guy? What new guy? You don't mean the little bald dude from Jordan, do you?"

"That's right."

"Great! Next I suppose you'll tell me you've booked a chariot limo, so I can leave in a blaze of glory!"

"You read my mind."

23

Go and Trash No More

A four-year-old kid thought she knew the Lord's Prayer. "And forgive us our trash baskets," she prayed, "as we forgive those who put trash in our baskets."

There's a lot of trash in our baskets. If not in our baskets, in our basements. No wonder we have a hard time walking about without tripping and falling when we are carrying so much garbage.

The first thing we need to understand about garbage is that garbage is very complex. Very deep. It is the stuff of Shakespeare: "Who steals my purse steals trash," quoth Iago to Othello, "but he that filches from me my good name/ robs me of that which not enriches him/ and makes me poor indeed." Like I said, deep.

Even the word is hard to spell. Usually the word is seen as in Garage Sale. We always forget to put in the *b*. As someone has observed, when have you ever been to a garage sale in which the garage has actually been for sale?

Garbage is also egalitarian: Everyone has it and everyone wants to get rid of it. According to a study by the National Solid Waste Management Association, we are producing so much garbage that most states unload their garbage on neighboring states. New York and New Jersey, for example, export 7.9 million tons of garbage each year. These two states alone provide enough garbage annually to fuel three Trident submarines for ten years or keep Congress in paper for 30 days.

The logic here requires us to understand that if some states are exporting garbage, others are importing garbage! Ohio leads the way, importing garbage from eight states, exporting to only five. Ohio clearly has an unfavorable balance of trash. It is the only state in the union that looks like my basement.

Nevada, Wyoming, and Utah keep all of their own garbage and import even more of it from other states. But consider Oregon and Washington: They are the only states that actually have a reciprocal trade agreement. Like two adolescents exchanging wet wads of chewing gum, they import and export garbage only with each other.

People are like this. The dumpers unload their emotional garbage on anyone and everyone. They're on *Jerry Springer* or *Geraldo*. They see themselves as victims and lose no time explaining why. They often assume a very self-righteous pose as they burden others with the garbage of their own cluttered lives.

Dumpees, on the other hand, can't seem to get enough garbage. They thrive on it, splashing about in other people's misery like pigs in manure. And when there isn't enough, these garbage-mongers create more of it and spread it around like rancid pâté. Their lives resemble the stark landscape of a toxic waste site. Nothing grows except bacteria and viruses, all the while leaking destructive carcinogens and acids into the societal bio-system. If you think that is harsh, consider the words of Jesus to the Pharisees: "You hypocrites. You are like whitewashed tombs, which look beautiful on the outside but on the inside are full of dead men's bones and everything unclean" (Matthew 23:27, NIV). He goes on to describe them as "snakes" and "vipers." The garbage the Pharisees carried around was the filthiness of their own self-righteousness.

Jesus is in the garbage disposal business! He has offered to freely take all of my cares, burdens, mistakes, fallings, and failures and separate me from them as far as the east is from the west!

There may be trash in my basket, but there doesn't need to be. Jesus says, "Go and trash no more!"

24

Sharks

When my youngest daughter graduated from high school, I sent her to Cozumel, Mexico, as a graduation present. Not alone. I went with her.

After we arrived on this beautiful island, her first stop was a Canadian hairdresser who put her blondish hair in Bo Derek braids and white beads. To go with her angel white swimsuit.

"I am her father," I said to the dark-skinned young men of San Miguel who inquired. "Would you like to be my father-in-law?" one replied in broken English, grinning. Within 24 hours of our arrival, Debbie had an international network of friends who were staying at different resorts on the island.

We met our first friends at Carlos 'N Charlie's, a local hot spot where one can sip colorful drinks, listen to the music, and dance. On our first visit, they had a contest for free margaritas. One simply had to keep a hula hoop going longer than anyone else. We watched for a while, and then Debbie slapped me on the back and said, "Well, dad, I'm gonna get you some free margaritas." And she did.

We met some friends who took scuba lessons so that they could enjoy the great diving off Palancar Reef. They told us that they had learned some underwater hand signals. The sign for shark is a karate chop to the forehead.

I adopted this signal with my daughter. As patrons of Carlos 'N Charlie's enjoyed themselves imbibing tequila and dancing, bumping and grinding, I noted grimly who my daughter had taken up with, or who was expressing interest. If I disapproved, I raised my salute and chopped my forehead in warning. Shark! Stay away from this sleazeball!

So we soaked up the sun and danced. Debbie has perfected the art of getting a tan into a science. Her beach towel always lies at proper angles relative to the solar orbit for maximum exposure. It is fruitless to warn her of gamma radiation, melanomas, and the like. So she worships the sun like a Mayan priestess, laying inert on the searing sand, headphones in her ears pumping Zhane, or Salt 'n Pepa's Very Necessary. She turns her body evenly like a bird on a rotisserie. I wonder if she will ever develop a taste for Mozart or Vivaldi. At night she danced, while I stood nearby with my shark salute at the ready.

In the rite of passage we call graduation, this child is now venturing into a world of both sun and sharks. Too much sun is not healthy, but one experience with a shark can destroy her. I remember when she phoned me frantically and said, "Dad, Colleen's been shot." Debbie made it to the hospital just before Colleen died. I listened numbly as she spoke at the memorial service for her friend, one of four victims of a pizza parlor massacre. I watched her weep and shared her frustration and anger with my Boomer Generation's utter ineptitude in dealing with the problems that plague us. I had hoped we could provide a better world for Debbie and her friends, a shark-free environment, or at least water that's safe to swim in.

I fear the sharks, but she laughs. She is getting a tan, she is living in the sun, she is a child of the light, and sun shines on her like the sparkle of a thousand waters.

We stayed in Cozumel for a week. We were at Carlos 'N Charlie's every night. Time enough to meet Stephen of Montreal, William of Chicago, Tom of Omaha, Lars of Sweden, Gunther of Germany, and Damian of San Miguel. Ah, Damian, the lad at Carlos 'N Charlie's who led the tequila dances, who winked his way into Debbie's heart. "Dad, he's got such a great smile!" The lad who already has a girlfriend. "It doesn't matter, Dad."

When we came home, I had a forehead crease a quarter inch deep.

25

Not Ready to Collapse My Tent

I know I shouldn't let it bother me. Turning fifty is no big deal. At the lead of the Boomer generation there are another 10 million just like me turning fifty and doing just fine, thank you very much. Excuse me, but I have grown progressively less fond of birthdays. They're like slalom markers on a downhill run: The closer you get to the end the faster they appear. I keep throwing away the solicitations I get in the mail from AARP, but they insist on sending them anyway.

I'm still attached to the forties: child, family, education, and vocation. Life has been a happy blend of youthful vigor and mid-life maturity. In my thirties I became a father for the last time; in my forties I became a G............ for the first time. Even as I write this, it doesn't seem real. I have this recurring nightmare: I am running a race against a biological clock, and losing; I get winded playing chess; I reach the top of the ladder only to find it's leaning against the wrong wall; my back goes out before I do; I look forward to a dull evening; my mind makes contracts that my body can't keep; my knees buckle, but my belt won't; I sit in a rocking chair, but can't get it going; a fortune teller offers to read my face. Had enough?

Old jokes; you've heard them before. But they underscore a troubling truth: I am getting old. I worry about getting everything accomplished in the time left. No gong has sounded, but upon turning fifty it appears I am moving from a decade of assurance, safety, and protection to one of uncertainty, postmodern angst, Boomer anxiety, doubts, and fears. Soon I will be thrust to the front of the "generational train." I am not sure I am ready for that responsibility.

At age forty, one is finally forced to differentiate between the age of the body and the age of the spirit. Until now, I have been able to insist that such a differentiation was unnecessary: Both spirit and body were youthful, energetic, and not yet actualizing their potential. Now I must admit that some polarization is taking place. The body is not that of a nineteen-year-old. I am tired of walking around sucking in the waistline. But is that inner person—what I call my spirit—sagging, too? Or has it instead retained its youthful vitality, remaining green, supple, and pliant, fed by the springs of wisdom and understanding? "Old age," said the early nineteenth-century theologian Friedrich Schleiermacher, "is an idle prejudice, an ugly fruit of the mad delusion that the spirit is dependent upon the body" (attribution untraced).

Never mind that he wrote that when he was thirty-five; at fifty I have decided to set my sights on the development of the spirit, that part of me time cannot touch. I cannot hope to escape the ravages of time unless I can see something of the timeless within myself. So I undertake a sort of spiritual pilgrimage, unfettered by time or age, aches or pains, until I reach the ultimate passage itself.

Hildegard of Bingen, an abbess and mystic of the late twelfth century, painted a scene in which she depicts all the potential and gifts of the human person within a tent that is folded up at birth. In life, one opens up the panels, sets up the tent, and explores the gifts within it.

At fifty I am still struggling to set up the tent. It sometimes collapses about me, and I often seem lost in despair within its folds. But mostly, I am at work fastening, securing, exploring, and delighting and frequently experiencing the "radical amazement" that Rabbi Heschel calls mysticism. I had always believed that if the time-honored bon mot was true that "life begins at forty" it surely must end at fifty. Now, however, I know that the quality of life is not solely dependent upon the health of the body but the vigor of the soul.

"Yes," says Schleiermacher, "in my advanced years I shall still have the same strength of spirit, and I shall never lose my keen zest for life."

Amen. Now would someone please hand me another tent pole?

How to Reach the Author

Timothy Merrill can be reached for information about speaking engagements at 2001 Bell Court, Denver, CO 80215-1713; Phone (303) 239-6550; Fax (303) 205-1061; E-mail: merrilltf@aol.com